INTERIORS
2nd BOOK
OF HOTELS

INTERIORS 2nd BOOK OF HOTELS

BY HENRY END

WHITNEY LIBRARY OF DESIGN,
an imprint of Watson-Guptill Publications/New York

For M.P.C.

"Deference is the instinctive respect which we pay to the great and the good—the unconscious acknowledgment of the superiority or excellence of others."

Tryoh Edwards (1809–1894)

Copyright© 1978 by Whitney Library of Design

First published 1978 in New York by Whitney Library of Design,
an imprint of Watson-Guptill Publications,
a division of Billboard Publications, Inc.,
1515 Broadway, New York, N.Y. 10036

Library of Congress Cataloging in Publication Data
End, Henry, 1915-
   Interiors 2nd book of hotels.
   Bibliography: p.
   Includes index.
   1. Hotels, taverns, etc. I. Title.
NA7800.E53   728.5   77-25036
ISBN O-8230-7281-9

Manufactured in U.S.A.

First Printing, 1978

Contents

Foreword

Originally a French word, "hotel" once meant "a town mansion, a large house; hall, viz., Hotel de Ville, city hall." The first large hospices for travelers, built in Washington, New York, and Boston a century or more ago, were called "hotels." These structures had no equivalent in Great Britain or in Europe at that time. Thus, when large American-type inns were built overseas, they were called hotels.

E. M. Statler is generally credited with having made a great contribution to the first truly modern hotels of the type now being built around the globe. The original Buffalo Statler, erected in 1907–1908, provided American travelers with such hitherto unknown conveniences as "a room and a bath for a dollar and a half" with telephones, circulating ice water, and a morning newspaper under the door. The Hotel Pennsylvania, opened in 1919, was virtually a city within a city so far as guest services were concerned. The front office system introduced by Statler in 1919 still constitutes today's method for handling reservations in most hotels, despite advances of the Computer Age. Fifty years after Statler's death, the hotels he built still compete with leading new hotels because the innovations he introduced became the standard.

However, our world is becoming more complex, and we in the hospitality industry must be prepared to consider a veritable upheaval in our thoughts and ideas as well as in our methods of operation. This calls for an evaluation and reappraisal of our traditional philosophies and concepts of construction and design.

Aside from labor, nonfunctional design is the factor most often pinpointed by operating management as causing inefficiencies in various operating departments. It is felt that too many mistakes make in the past are still being designed into today's facilities and that insufficient attention is being paid to traffic patterns within the hotel. More emphasis in the future will be placed on designing hotels and motels from the "inside out" rather than upon architectural concepts of exterior design.

Henry End has come to grips with these problems of traditionalism and herewith presents a most interesting and worthwhile concept of what is, in my opinion, a much needed dimension in the field of hotel construction and design.

Robert A. Beck, Dean
School of Hotel Administration
Cornell University

Preface

Before the troubles began in Lebanon, I spent a day of meetings at the Phoenicia where I was staying. Afterwards, I decided to take a stroll by the bay which flanks the hotel. Coming across what seemed for Beirut a well-stocked bookstore, I wandered inside to browse in the English book section. Much to my surprise, they were heavily stocked with an incredibly varied list of titles on art, design, and architecture. Also included was an out-of-print volume of my first *Interiors* book on hotels published in 1963. As I thumbed through the illustrations it appeared obvious that hotels built since 1963 had made giant steps in both directions.

I paid the equivalent of $30 for the book (published in the U.S. for $16.50) and returned to the Phoenicia to spend that evening in an objective appraisal of what I had written more than ten years previously.

While it was evident that a great deal of my design philosophy had not radically changed, the book as a whole was hopelessly out of date. Design concepts and building and furnishing costs had vastly changed. Several hotel chains important in 1963 were now extinct, while obscure hotel companies at the time of publication were now worldwide giants. The potential of the Middle East had not yet been discovered as a vast source of new hotel development. A new breed of imaginative designers were creating extravagant concepts—palaces and vacation resorts for the people and for young people too, as evidenced by the enormous appeal of Club Mediterranean. The book offered little indepth technical data and useful information for the designer or hotel operator embarking on a first hotel venture. I therefore felt a great deal of gratitude and relief when my publishers agreed that an updated, second edition was needed.

It might be possible, but it would be unreasonable to thank everyone who has contributed to this book. There are a few I cannot help but single out for special gratitude. Marion Page with professional skill unscrambled the miles of taped interviews, compiling, rewriting, and coordinating the pot-pourri of my thoughts, opinions, and experiences.

A designer associate suggested that it was a question of "those who know don't tell and those who tell don't know." This cynical view I found untrue. Of the many busy hotel executives and designers I contacted, very few indeed were not available for comment. Sir Charles Forte, head of the world's largest hotel chain, gave of his valuable time, and when played back, his tape alone could have filled a fair-size book. Peter di Tullio, President of Hyatt International, was at all times available to feed generous spoonfuls out of the bowl of his vast experience, as did his Executive Vice-President, Waggi Hanna, who provided Hyatt's technical standards and documentation. Sheraton's Robert Kittner gave generously of his time and technical information of enormous significance.

Others to whom I am indebted are the many designers who supplied their precious photographs. Alexander George and Ben Martin, two superb photographers, spent valuable time sorting out suitable subject material from their vast library of negatives.

Most helpful too were the hotel chains' public relations staffs, of whom a special thank you is extended to Georgia Beach, the super P.R. head of Hyatt International.

A special indebtedness goes to the staff of The Whitney Library of Design, particularly, Sarah Bodine and Susan Davis, who accomplished with a minimum of wasted effort and a maximum effect the difficult task of long distance tying together of loose ends of an incredible variety.

I also acknowledge with unlimited gratitude, Ruth Abreu, my office manager for the past 15 years, who as usual throughout was a pillar of strength, putting up with a book intruding into her everyday workload.

In conclusion, my thanks to Sandra Kind, who typed and collated the manuscripts and burdensome correspondence with patience and diligence.

Introduction

Fifteen years have passed since the publication of my first book, *Interiors Book of Hotels and Motor Hotels.* That was a different time, a different era.

A decade and a half ago, we had no inkling of the enormous growth of tourism that was to come. Not in our wildest dreams did we anticipate that the Middle East would become a dynamic center of hotel growth. And that entity we call the Third World had not yet signaled that it would burst upon us.

In one short, tumultuous period the hotel industry has undergone as many changes and as many upheavals as this unstable globe itself. A new breed of architects and interior designers, virtually unknown when my book was written, are leading us into yet another decade of change.

All this excitement has not come about without the toppling of great names and the emergence of new ones. Important hotel chains have come to the fore, while we have seen the demise or deterioration of what were once highly respected ones.

For instance, fifteen years ago I considered the Nile Hilton "the jewel of the East" and gave it prominence in the first book. In Cairo alone, where Welton Becket set new standards of good hotel design and efficiency, the Nile Hilton was a citadel of the best in contemporary hotel design. Today Cairo boasts more than 10,000 new hotel rooms. There are 9 major hotels under construction and 22 planned in addition to the completed Sheraton and Meridian.

Saudi Arabia, that vast oil-rich desert country with a population of no more than 6 million, has 18 hotels under construction or in the planning stages. The picture is similar throughout the Middle East. Even Mecca has not been overlooked. Inter-Continental opened its doors to pilgrims in the Holy City in 1975.

The Iron Curtain has been breached with ease. Countries such as Hungary and Yugoslavia are spotted with the towers of modern hotels rising above ancient cities. Inter-Continental, the hotel division of Pan American Airlines, is adding to its worldwide holdings with hotels everywhere. Hilton International, the overseas symbol of the U.S. traveler, is a password to convenience all over the globe.

In the light of all this activity, one may very well ask about the spectre of overbuilding. Unfortunately, it has arrived along with the good things that have happened, most noticeably in Great Britain. The British government in 1967 in an all-out endeavor to lure more tourists, embarked on a generous scheme of grants designed to assist hotel developers. The result was disastrous. Badly planned hotels in unlikely locations were embraced by inexperienced hotel operators. Many of these hotel companies were in bankruptcy or facing liquidation. Miraculously, the last two years have shown the highest occupancy in history due to the oil-rich Middle East tourist. Nevertheless, it is hoped that this new book will in some way help to head off such possible pitfalls.

In preparation of the material, many taped interviews were made with international leaders in the various branches of the hotel field. Managing executives, food and beverage consultants, hotel owners, and technical service planning personnel were invited to give their views. Not forgotten was the most important member of the design team—the architect.

Of all the things that have occurred during the last 15 years, perhaps nothing is more important to hotel people than the new role of the architect in hotel design. Once the nemesis of the interior designer, the architect has become a keystone of any well-thought-out hotel design undertaking.

John Portman, for example, has demonstrated that total design by a well-disciplined architectural organization can result in a totally exciting experience. The Rome-and-London-based Rader Mileto, a spinoff of Gropius Group, is not only sympathetic to the interior designer's role, but is willing to create an architectural cocoon for the internal space without ignoring the esthetic quality of the architecture as a whole. Architectural firms have become aware that what occurs within the hotel's walls can spell profit or loss for the management.

Thankfully in the U.S., the hotel operator has come of age, esthetically speaking. Whereas it was once virtually impossible for a designer to "sell" a contemporary interior, however modern the exterior, many international hotel operators now recognize that today's affluent and younger traveling public will accept contemporary interiors gratefully.

There are exceptions, as there always are. The giant, influential Holiday Inns firm continues to export its Memphis kitsch to the ends of the earth. In sharp contrast, Holiday Inns' Canadian affiliates have executed many commendable interiors.

In the following pages we will deal with many approaches to hotel interiors. I intend to make my own conclusions as objective and constructive as possible, dealing mainly with the values that make for good merchandising, good design principles, and suitable maintenance standards.

In an era in which, particularly in America, less has become better, boosterism has withered, and the millionth citizen is no longer the Chamber of Commerce's most cherished goal, the hotel industry is flourishing and growing, getting bigger and bigger, and marking up new achievements in its record book.

The Marriotts have added giant convention motor hotels in Denver and Miami and thousand-room monsters in Los Angeles and New Orleans and are now established overseas. Hyatt, a relatively new innkeeper, made its big splash with the Regency Atlanta, an architectural triumph, and is pushing ahead with other spectacular buildings. Not to be outdone, Disney World in Orlando, Florida, has three breathtaking hotels, one of which is shown on page 57.

What does all this mean to the architect, owner, and interior designer of hotels? How will the designer cope with the technological breakthrough in building construction, the ever-increasing cost of building, and outmoded building codes? Is the preengineered and packaged building unit the answer?

Many of these questions are already answered in existing operations and more are being solved on the drawing boards. This book will demonstrate what's happening with this vast and shifting scene and show what some designers and farsighted management teams are striving to do. No crystal ball gazing will be resorted to. We intend to grapple with hard facts.

Woodcut of the Grand Court of the Palace Hotel in San Francisco in 1878. Courtesy Bettmann Archives.

1. Why a Hotel

The modern hotel is an American invention as surely as the skyscraper, the movie palace, and the hot dog are. In 1821 an English journalist noted that if a traveler complained of American inns and hinted his dislike of sleeping four to a bed, he was told to wait 100 years and see their superiority to the British. The prediction turned out to be amazingly conservative. Less than 10 years after the Englishman made his observation, the Tremont House, that prototype of the modern American hotel, appeared in Boston to enchant all who visited it. The Tremont was designed by Isaiah Rogers and its cornerstone, appropriately enough, was laid on the Fourth of July, 1828.

There were many reasons why the modern hotel got its start in the U.S. It was a mobile society then as now. Between 1830 and 1930 a great system of railroad trains, river, lake, and coastal steamers, gave the country the finest public transportation in the world. In 1883, the *Hotel Gazette* estimated there were more than 200,000 commercial travelers in the U.S. In 1904 Henry James was tempted to ask "if the hotel-spirit may not just *be* the American spirit most seeking and finding itself."

What is a hotel today? It is certainly not the ferry tavern of the 17th century where several overnight guests were apt to find themselves sharing the same bed, nor is it the Cincinnati hotel of the 1830s that Mrs. Trollope reported in her *Domestic Manners of the Americans* was "neat and comfortable enough" but "devoid of nearly all the accommodation that Europeans conceive necessary to decency and comfort." Neither is it the 18th-century City Tavern in Philadelphia where "in order to better accommodate Strangers," its owner "fitted up several elegant bed rooms, detached from noise, and as private as a lodging house." The City Tavern boasted a "Genteel Coffee-Room . . . properly supplied with English and American papers and magazines." And even John Adams relates that he "could not resist the importunity to go to the tavern, the most genteel one in America. . . . After some time spent in conversation," he continues, "a curtain was drawn and in the other half of the chamber a supper appeared as elegant as ever was laid on a table."

The modern hotel of today is an extraordinarily complicated machine, a city within a city, and a direct descendant of that triumph of the 1820s—the Tremont House in Boston designed by Rogers and hailed by European and American visitors alike as one of the wonders of its age. Behind its chaste Greek Revival facade, it boasted astonishingly functional planning, not to mention the most advanced plumbing and other amenities. There was a central rotunda and acres of gilded public space, elaborate bathrooms, free soap in every room, and a lock on every door. For the first time in America, if not in the world, as Talbot Hamlin says, "mechanical equipment became an important element in architectural design." Dickens found the Tremont "excellent," noting that it had "more galleries, colonnades, piazzas, and passages than I can remember, or the reader would believe." Julia Ward Howe's father found it too luxurious for decent people. But only a few years later Rogers' world-famed Astor House opened in New York with even more wondrous innovations.

The facilities and amenities of the Tremont and the Astor, as Henry-

A hotel is a theater experience. The space should create an emotional involvement. Public areas, restaurants, and guest rooms make up the theater and set the stage for the dramas that unfold. And the guest is both the audience and the participant in this hotel experience.

Howard Hirsch

Russell Hitchcock points out in his essay on "American Influence Abroad," "were of a completeness hardly known up to this time in foreign hostelries. The evidence of this influence is as clear as the current international use of the term 'motel.'" The great hotels of the 1860s building boom in England, adds Hitchcock, "were not more complete without a 'grand American bar' than they would be today. Among other ideas from America was the inclusion of a barbershop, or 'hair-cutting saloon," described in the account in the *Illustrated London News* of the International Hotel in London in 1858 as 'another American luxury.'"

It is not surprising that Rogers has been called the father of the modern hotel. There was a demand and he answered it. Cities were growing and with them a need for better accommodations for transients than those provided by taverns. Isaiah Rogers met that need with his "People's Palaces."

But in spite of all the plush, plumbing, "perpendicular railways," and other creature comforts, Rogers' job was a lot easier than that of today's hotel designer. No feasibility study was necessary in the 1820s. There was a need and Yankee ingenuity did the rest.

What America begat before the middle of the 19th century will surely reach its ultimate in prepackaged rooms and prepackaged meals before the end of the 20th century. It may be a dismal thought, but it is efficient and it is an economic necessity which is probably the end result of American know-how.

Today, says Hilton International president Charles Bell, there is little difference between what is considered an American hotel and a European hotel. American hotel methods have taken over. In fact, most builders or international developers seek an American hotel management company.

CREATING THE PROJECT

The why of a hotel in the 1970s is not unlike the why of a hotel in the 1830s, but everything about it has become far more complicated—its inception, its financing, its designing, its planning, its building, its operating. It has been said that hotels and hospitals are the most difficult buildings to design. But probably hotels are even more difficult than hospitals because they must have built-in sales appeal. Americans are still travelers and there are many more of them. They can go much farther in much less time. They have, moreover, been joined in their mobile traits by the citizens of most other developed countries in the world. Today's hotel guests, whether businesspeople or vacationers, are more demanding and their tastes are more divergent. They expect certain standards. All this, of course, not only creates a need for guest rooms for transients but a need for convention and banqueting facilities. The "People's Palaces" of the 19th century soon became the social centers of our cities and to a certain degree they still are. In the Middle East, with all its new money, one of the priorities is for hotels that will provide that kind of credence and importance within a community.

A variety of factors may suggest the need for building a hotel in a certain place. There may be a lack of hotel rooms and convention facilities. Or there may be an important sports event or international fair on the agenda. Many smaller U.S. cities, like those in the Middle East, want to build hotels to enhance their urban image for political reasons or because they want to become convention centers. Each of these reasons had its 19th-century American precedents. A tremendous number of hotels were built in New York in the years immediately preceding the Crystal Palace exhibition of 1853 because it was thought that America's first World's Fair would draw large crowds to the city. And not long after the Tremont opened, it was an accepted theory that no city amounts to anything unless it has at least one hotel which can give visitors a favorable impression of the city's greatness, enterprise, and hospitality.

None of these reasons in themselves, however, is enough to produce a

Above: View of Boston's Tremont House, the prototype of the modern American hotel, built in the late 1820s. Courtesy Bettmann Archives.

Below: Lithograph of the Astor House of the 1860s located in New York's financial district. Courtesy Bettmann Archives.

13

Woodcut of the vestibule and office of the Grand
Pacific Hotel in Chicago. Courtesy Bettmann
Archives.

successful hotel today. There were almost no modern hotels in Egypt until a short time ago. Soon there will be an overabundance. Waves of hotels were built for the Munich Olympics. Now they are half empty.

So the "why" of a hotel today has to be based on something more than guesswork, nationalism, or egotism.

MARKET RESEARCH

Long before the design team comes into being, many behind-the-scenes activities take place which the designer should be aware of. Contrary to public opinion, few of the properties that operate under the banner of the well-known hotel chains are owned outright by the companies which manage them. These giant chains, with certain exceptions, have a management contract with the owning company for a prescribed number of years based on a percentage of earnings.

Before any decision is made to build a hotel, an owning company—be it an individual, a corporation, or even a government agency—usually employs one of the internationally established accounting firms, such as Horwath & Horwath or Harris-Kerr-Forster, to study the feasibility of constructing a hotel in a particular place. Sometimes a hotel chain will make its own feasibility study. But no matter who makes it, the study will check out local competition; revenues of competing hotels based on occupancy, food and beverage sales; and whether the proposed hotel will be able to fill a particular need. For example, there may be an overabundance of hotel rooms in a certain area but no one hotel that can provide the facilities for large conventions. Obviously a new hotel with such facilities would have distinct advantages over its competition. People who attend conventions usually prefer to spend the night and eat their meals in the hotel where the convention meetings are taking place.

A feasibility study will provide an analysis of profit forecast which is vital to ensure that the investment is not only sound but practical. Land cost related to the total investment will be an important factor in this study. Ever-increasing costs of constructing and operating a hotel are paramount in predicting the projected profit of a hotel.

Under the heading of "Interpretation and Evaluation of Data," the *Architects Journal*'s book on the *Principles of Hotel Design* lists the following points to be determined if a hotel is to be profitable:

1. Demand for hotel facilities, accommodation, and catering.

2. Degree to which present facilities meet the demand.

3. What the future position is likely to be.

4. What the corresponding opportunities are at the various levels of demand, based on displacement created, transient and future.

Since feasibility studies are based on facts and not imagination, it is sometimes possible to come up with the wrong answer. The feasibility study for John Portman's spectacularly successful Hyatt Regency in Atlanta was negative. But Hyatt, with no prestige hotels at the time, was willing to take the risk. Hotel executives don't usually want to take avoidable risks. A formula has to reach obsolescence before they will try something different. But of course a formula can sometimes be an asset, such as the orange roof used by the Howard Johnson chain, which is easily identifiable and tells the potential guest what to expect.

Even if the feasibility study is positive, there is still no guarantee of success. An imaginative approach is also needed. Writing in the June 1976 *Hospitality,* C. DeWitt Coffman, president of the Coffman Corporation in Miami, consultants and troubleshooters for hotels and resorts, points out that if a hotel is to be successful today, it must be distinctive in some particular way. It must have a unique personality, special features, or something that sets it apart from other hotels and will not only bring guests back, but prompt them to recommend it to their friends. Design, as the Atlanta Hyatt Regency has shown, is a strong contributing factor to

Understanding the people problems in our building designs starts with the earliest examination of the requirements which form the program, the concept of the spaces, their functions, their human touches. . . . We want the interior staff to amalgamate with the architectural team in these early stages and stay with the process until the design is frozen.

Vincent G. Kling, AIA

Above: Formal gardens enhance the Ponce de Leon Hotel in St. Augustine, Florida, in the 1880s. Courtesy Bettmann Archives.

Right: The sitting room of the United States Hotel in Saratoga, New York. Courtesy Bettmann Archives.

that kind of distinction. Hotel developers and operators, Coffman suggests, should ask themselves why their logical potential customers would rather stay in this particular hotel than somewhere else. Then, he advises, "build into your building what the customers want. Color, design, space, warmth. Then stir in friendliness and willingness to serve and things to do. Then add in action and fun. Mix well, and you'll probably come up with an operation with some personality and charm."

He cautions, however, that "unless you're designing a cadaver, don't just copy all the other motels spraddled across America. Plan your own distinctive operation, with its own character, with special come-ons. Build in the physical assets and the intangible service factors that people who make up your various logical market tell you they want and need.

"Nuts to nothingness," continues Coffman. 'You've gotta have your own special somethingness—whether it's architecture, decor, an Acapulco-type pool, or a whole building that revolves so that every room has a view of sunrise or sunset, or a super-swinging bar, or mirrors on the bedroom ceiling. Anything at all, just so it's not just another cold, lifeless, unimaginative, drab rectangular blob with no action, no warmth, no friendliness."

It was certainly the "special somethingness" of the 19th-century Tremont as well as the 20th-century Hyatt Regency that have made them so newsworthy and so popular.

ASSEMBLING THE HOTEL PACKAGE

Once a hotel has a site, it has the financing requirements under control. Financing may be derived from many sources—insurance institutions or possibly a group of business leaders in the community. Banks are not usually interested in long-term financing. Sometimes grants from government agencies are available, such as those made possible by the United Kingdom's Development of Tourism Act of 1969, which provided cash grants and loans for the building of new hotels in the U.K. The aim was to encourage immediate investment in hotels and corresponding increase in accommodations.

Interestingly enough, another source of financing can emanate from large construction companies. Bechtel International, based in San Francisco but concentrating most of its activities overseas, will finance, build, equip, furnish, and employ the design and engineering team to produce a "turnkey" hotel for the operator. Many hotels of the Inter-Continental chain have been established in this manner. Cementation, a United Kingdom-based company and a division of Trafalgar House which also has Cunard among its conglomerate holdings, is another company specializing in that activity. Coutinho Caro Ltd., whose worldwide activities stem from its parent offices in Hamburg and London, is still another.

The hotel franchise is a phenomena of the past 20 years. Holiday Inns, for instance, owns and franchises more than 1,700 hotels in countries throughout the world. The franchise concept makes it possible for an individual or corporation to become a hotel owner without prior experience in the hotel field. Under a franchise arrangement, Holiday Inns will design, equip, furnish, staff, and operate the hotel (sharing, of course, in the profits) after establishing a predetermined sum for operating costs. The main advantage to the owner is the builtin referral system. But while all seems fair and advantageous to the owning company, much disenchantment has occurred. There has been little control, for example, over the erection of competing Holiday Inns in the immediate vicinity of an existing property. Holiday Inns, moreover, gained their reputation for being modest and thus cannot increase their rates in the face of rising construction costs. Their image, in other words, is Chevrolet, but building costs are Rolls Royce. Since brick and mortar costs are fixed, one might as well build a five-star as a two-star hotel.

We need turning more and more to the way people respond to a space than to the beautiful photograph which may or may not be available of that space. It is important to me to open up peoples' ideas on living, whether it be in public spaces or private residences. Many of the patterns which we've developed for living have little or nothing to do with the way in which we actually use a space.

Barry Brukoff

LIAISON BETWEEN INVESTOR AND ARCHITECT

It is essential that the architect first ascertain that a feasibility study has been made. Then it will be required to make design studies showing the best use of the site, together with sufficient descriptive and visual material for submission to the finance lending institution. This design service is usually paid for in a lump fee, without obliging the owner to the continued service of the designer. If the proposed hotel does become a financial reality, the architect who made the study is the most likely candidate to contract for the total design. Thus although a design study including expensive renderings and a scale model (an area in which no designer should economize) may not be profitable, it is often a worthwhile investment.

Rarely in the past has the interior designer been brought into these early stages of conceptual design. However, that situation is changing fast. Our office has been called in on several occasions to team up with a total environmental design team—the architect, landscape architect, engineers, graphic and lighting designers, et al.—for a complete conceptual presentation. Methods and techniques of presentation will be dealt with in Chapter 7.

The soaring atrium of the Hyatt Regency Atlanta.

2. The Design Team

"The single discipline firm is a twentieth-century phenomenon," points out Kenneth Walker of the Walker-Grad Partnership. "When you look at older structures, like the cathedral at Chartres and the Farnese Palace, you see an integral tie between art and architecture. In those times, the architect was the organizer and overseer of the crafts people."

If the complex hotel of today is to be successful, it will require the teamwork of many disciplines. I don't believe the interior designer's responsibility is restricted to the interiors. I think the design team, and I want to emphasize *design team*, has to work together on the exterior and interior of a hotel. "A building is not complete," as William Pulgram, AIA, president of Associated Space Design Inc., puts it, "until the interior spaces are done. Most of the design today is a result of team planning."

The design team includes the architect, engineers, interior designer, landscape architect, and lighting designer, among other specialists. All of them have to work together on the total design. The most successful hotels are those in which the exterior and interior spaces work in conjunction. If there is a landscape architect, he of course is responsible for the exterior spaces, but his work can't be wholly successful unless it is related to the exterior and the interior of the hotel. This is especially true when there are outdoor facilities such as restaurants and pool areas.

The architect is usually the first member of the design team who is commissioned by the management group or the owner. But once the financing has been set and the hotel is to be developed, the interior designer should be retained. The interior designer can never get into the project too soon. The novice owner doesn't understand this and sometimes makes the mistake of waiting until the building is underway before the interior designer is brought in, which may even necessitate remodeling prior to opening. The large hotel chains, however, are well aware of lining up the interior designer early. When Robert Kittner of the Sheraton Management Corporation was asked what problems he encountered when working with interior designers, he replied that the problem was more often with the client "who doesn't bring the interior designer on board soon enough, resulting in all sorts of traumatic experiences when the interior designer tries to do his thing." Kittner added that he believes "extreme flexibility is required between the interior designer and the architect and the client to achieve their mutual purpose." He particularly criticized the client who doesn't know what he wants "before the design team is turned on."

If an architectural firm has total design ability, it will sometimes attempt to sell an entire design package—architecture, engineering, interior design, et al. The disadvantage of this is that the architecture is the tail wagging the dog. I believe that the interiors of a hotel are really important to the public—and the public is the interior designer's main concern. The architect is concerned with the total esthetic effect, but an interior designer might put spaces in a building that are unrelated to the architecture, such as a night club or other facility that has its own environment. From the viewpoint of the owner and operator, however, there

We foresee increasing involvement of architectural teams, including interior designers, in the total environment to be created in and around a structure or other facilities. An architect views a project in more encompassing terms than an interior designer. The designer works with details. They complement each other. The change will be more and more generally to include interior designers in the architectural team, so that they will become involved in the evolution of architectural space rather than merely in decorating it. They will have a much closer relationship with architects. More design divisions will be built into architectural firms. The day of the decorator is passing. More and more the significant results will be achieved by interior designers working hand-in-glove with architects.

Vincent Kling, AIA

IDS Center in Minneapolis, Minnesota, is a complex of four buildings, a 51-story office tower, an 8-story office annex, a 2-story store building, and the Marquette Inn (shown here), all built around this enclosed, parklike Crystal Court which the hotel utilizes as a lobby. The hotel's hanging garden restaurants overlook the Crystal Court.

Above: Bedrooms are on three sides of a planted court at the Airport Hotel in Dublin, Ireland; this corridor forms the fourth side.

Right: The ceiling lends drama to the ballroom and reception area of the Gulf Hotel in Muscat.

Our best answer to date has been the systems approach: utilizing team members of many disciplines to solve a given design problem. Most designers have accepted the validity of the systems approach. Putting it into practice though, brings up a whole new set of problems; communication barriers, difficulties in understanding professional jargon and the techniques of group interaction, ego conflicts.

Regina Baraban, Editor, *Designer* Magazine

is probably an advantage in having all services emanating from one office.

The hotel operator's only concern is that the design does what he wants it to do—sell the interiors as a merchandising tool. The guest's main concern is that he feels comfortable inside the hotel. He rarely pays any attention to its exterior, particularly if it is in a city hemmed in by other buildings. Even when Dickens visited Boston in the 1830s, he had a lot to say about the interior of the Tremont but little about its Greek Revival exterior. "Unless a building is efficient, pleasant, and comfortable for its occupants," says Louis Beal, executive vice president of Interior Space Design in the July 1975 *AIA Journal,* "it doesn't work no matter how well it may look to the person walking around it."

Norman Anderson, president of Gulf Hotels (a hotel management company and division of Gulf Airlines), puts it this way: "A hotel should be designed from the inside out. It has to be designed entirely from the operational point of view." As an interior designer, I of course believe this is true. It is my feeling that although the exterior of the hotel should be attractive, it is really not important. The merchandising of a hotel exists mainly inside, except in the case of a resort hotel where there are certain outside features, such as pool areas.

Detail of Gulf Hotel ceiling.

All this suggests that the interior designer may be the most important member of the hotel design team, but it should always be remembered that it is a team and it should operate as a team. While the architect and interior designer may not have a contract with each other, both sides need to have a total understanding of the project. Good design in hotels, says architect Patrick B. Garnett in the English magazine *Interior Design,* "must of necessity be that concerned with solving spatial and circulation problems—connected with guests arriving and leaving, service deliveries being made, cooking, eating and drinking all taking place in different areas at the same time." The designer, Garnett adds, "must also ensure that the most pleasing visual effects are achieved by the careful use of materials, in lighting and in giving design consideration to every item—down to graphics, planting, and display." In the hotel, he says, "The plan must work from the beginning and must dictate the outward form of the building. This requires an understanding by the architect of the way a hotel functions."

A design team that works together on all aspects of the building from the beginning to the end may well be the key to the successful hotel of the future. "To create a hotel that is unique within itself and not simply like the last, the design team should develop a spirit for the hotel," says Thomas Hughes, a vice president of ISD Inc., in the February 1976 *Architectural Record.* "This spirit should evolve out of the design process; it should not be affected or superimposed on the interiors of a building. If the design team analyzes the community and its history, the site, the economics of the project, types of construction available to the locale, the time frames to be met and other formulating influences, this 'spirit' will rise naturally from its beginnings."

To put it in the simplest terms, it might be a landscape architect's task to create the site plan; an architect's task to fit the hotel sympathetically into that plan, to reflect regional character, and to create a shell for the necessary interior functions; and the interior designer's task to create congenial interiors that fit their function, but it is the team effort that endows the entire project with the kind of distinction that marks the successful hotel.

INTERIOR DESIGNER'S RESPONSIBILITIES

Most contracts are made with the owner. Hotel management companies rarely enter into a contract directly with the interior designer or the architect, but they usually recommend the architect and interior designer to the client who is the owner. While we deal directly with the client, we are really working through the offices of the management company for whom the client is building the hotel in accordance with the management company's requirements.

If the owner or client has had previous experience with hotels, he will understand something about fees. If not, he is assisted by the hotel chain. Hilton, Hyatt International, Inter-Continental, Sheraton, among other large hotel chains, have their own technical services, and they stipulate the program of services to be performed by the interior designer.

The technical services provided by Hyatt under the direction of Wagih Hanna, as outlined below, are similar to those provided by most hotel chains:

1. Assist the design team, at the master plan level, in the selection of sites appropriate to the development of the hotel structures.

2. Prepare a detailed project description for the hotels including the interior design themes therein.

3. Prepare a complete breakdown of space allocations of all areas of the proposed hotels.

4. Provide architectural and engineering standards as well as design criteria applicable to this project.

5. Work with the design team to develop architectural concepts that would reflect the programmatic intent as well as the operational requirements.

6. Develop the necessary layouts for all the hotel special areas, such as front desks, administrative offices, back-of-the-house and personnel facilities.

7. Coordinate, at every phase of development of the project, the performances of all special consultants, such as kitchen and laundry consultants, lighting designers, etc., with the development of the project by the various disciplines.

8. Supervise the preparation of the design development and working drawings and specifications (including those for architectural, structural, mechanical, and electrical systems): interior and graphic designs; and design and standards for furniture, furnishings, fixtures, and equipment.

9. Monitor the project during the design development, interior design, and work drawings stages for the purposes of achieving cost control and operational efficiency of the hotel layout.

10. Assist the design team in the selection of all the architectural finishes and provide site inspection services during construction, to ascertain that the design intent is being respected.

Generally, if the scope of the job can be clearly defined, we charge a percentage. If the scope is somewhat nebulous, we charge for time and materials.

Warren Platner, FAIA

After the program of services to be performed by the interior designer is formulated, an agreement is worked out. A straight fee is the usual arrangement with designers, while architects generally work on a percentage of the cost of the building or a fixed fee, which is predicated on the amount of public space and the number of guest rooms.

For a medium-to-luxury hotel based on 1977 costs, for example, the public space might cost $700,000, with 500 guest rooms at the cost of $3,000 per room (including corridors), for a total of $2,200,000. For a 500-room hotel, you can take 15 percent of the FFE (furniture, fixtures, and equipment) for the public space. Fifteen percent of $700,000 is $105,000, and then you add about 50 percent of the guest room cost, which is approximately $150,000. The total fee would then be $255,000.

Unfortunately, the 300-room hotel takes as much work as the 500-room hotel because the public spaces are approximately the same size and the design emphasis is in the public spaces. The design of the guest rooms is repetitious, and it doesn't make much difference whether there are 300 or 500 of them. (The percentage should really be higher for a smaller hotel.) So the fee for a 1,000-room hotel might not be much greater than for a

The entrance, lobby, and mezzanine of the Bristol Place in Toronto, Canada.

Right: Shopping arcade in the Hyatt Regency Caspian Hotel in Chalus, Iran, is along the corridor leading to the coffee shop.

Below: Shopping arcade in the Nassau Beach Hotel, a resort and convention hotel in Nassau, West Indies.

500-room hotel. It might be 7 percent of the guest rooms and 10 percent of the public space, which makes a total of $280,000.

We are, however, talking about 1977. Design office costs in the last year have increased from 15 to 20 percent, so while these are guidelines, they have to be related to the cost of running an office and the cost of designers and other personnel. The ratio for gauging the office costs is three times the payroll. In other words if a designer is earning $15 per hour, the charge should be $45. Theoretically this should give the company a gross profit of 20 percent, which is in accordance with good accounting practice. This ratio doesn't relate to efficiency, however, since some design organizations can work much faster and perhaps more efficiently than others.

Although most contracts are based on experience, the American Institute of Architects and the American Society of Interior Designers have given a great deal of thought to working out standard contracts for interior design services which both architects and interior designers can use. Some of the forms are shown in Chapter 10 on pages 171–215.

Any contract is as good as the intent, and no better, and it should be fair to both parties. If the client doesn't want to pay you after three months and it ends up in litigation, the only person who will gain is the legal advisor. The danger of using a lawyer to draw up a contract is that he will come up with a document that is so binding that it won't be signed until the client has his own lawyer scrutinize it, resulting in a legal battle of wits.

The designer has to make certain that payments are kept up to date, and the most acceptable way we have found is by progressive payments. Let's assume the contract is for $200,000 and the retainer is 20 percent, which amounts to $40,000. The balance of $160,000 may have to be spread over a period of three years. It should then be divided into the number of months to completion. If it is done on a monthly basis, it is fairly easy to keep track of payments. If, for example, we had a half-million-dollar project to complete over a 6-month period, how much inflow of cash would we have every month? First, we would try to obtain a substantial retainer, a deposit. Then we would decide how many people we would need for the project—the type of personnel and the length of time. We would appoint a job captain who would be monitored by the designer-in-chief or company director. The job captain, in turn, would have other people working under him. He might be the outside person who is in contact with the client on site. Working as his backup within the organization would include production designers, draftspeople, graphic designer, lighting designer, personnel familiar with furniture selection, and so on. We would have to price the project in accordance with the length of time it would take to complete, the number of people needed and the cost of that personnel, and then multiply the payroll by three in order to arrive at our fee. Let's say there were three people earning $20,000 a year. That would be $10,000 each over a 6-month period and $30,000 for all three. That amount is then multiplied by three.

We don't strive, however, for a percentage return on every assignment. There is a lot of give and take. We may, for instance, have six projects in the house at one time, two of which may be extremely difficult and costly, and consequently unprofitable. But there may be another one or two that are more easy going and profitable. There are many reasons why some commissions are difficult and others easy. One may take longer to complete for a number of reasons. There may be others that are carefully programmed with competent contractors. We have to watch time records to check how much time we have devoted to a job. That helps in bidding on new projects. A design office is a feast or famine situation. All firms dealing creatively have their ups and downs.

You should be able to make 10 percent on all projects. Calculating costs on a time basis is usually preferable to a fixed fee, since you can't lose money this way and don't have to wait for payment until completion of the project.

Louis Beal

We talk out of three sides of our mouths, promising things we are not capable of fulfilling. I think 95 percent of the people in this business are emulators. Instead of analyzing they just keep copying. So few designers will put themselves out on a limb and fight to create something special. There has been very little real growth. Most designers operate on a commission, or kickback basis, and will specify where they get the biggest kickback. How can you do a good job for a client when you are getting money from the other side? Nobody can function well working for two concerns simultaneously. What happens when they conflict? The whole scene is bad; I think we should have a uniform way of charging.

Josephine Sokolski

Art Nouveau entrance to the Sheraton Atlanta's disco.

There is another way of handling a contract which we don't approve of, although we sometimes have to abide by it. That is receiving payment after certain phases of services have been performed. The problem with that type of contract is that there is no real breakoff period for each phase of a project; there may be situations when we are still working on phase one although phase two is in progress, and while working on the second phase, we may already be on phase three. But while phases are clearer cut in architecture, they can't be easily defined in interior design. So, this form of contract is more often used by architects.

One of the biggest problems in a design office is lack of sufficient cash to pay fixed expenses and salaries. If a designer has to wait a long time for payments as in the phase-type of contract, this can be particularly troublesome. Therefore I prefer monthly payments flowing in from each job so that income and expenses are predictable.

After agreeing to a contract for, say, $200,000 and then finding the cost will exceed this amount, a designer is obligated to honor the contract. If, however, there is evidence that the job is continuing at a deficit and the client is reasonable, some adjustment can usually be made. For example, we have contracted for projects that have taken a great deal longer than the contract called for. There may be strikes, lack of material, unexpected local conditions, an inefficient building contractor, lack of funds, mechanical or structural problems—any number of reasons—that may stretch a 2-year program into 3 or 4 years.

There are, however, many ways to handle contracts. Generally, says Warren Platner, FAIA, "If the scope of the job can be clearly defined we charge a percentage. If the scope is somewhat nebulous, we charge for time and materials."

MEETING WITH CLIENTS/MANAGEMENT

It is important to establish a good rapport with clients and accept the way they operate. But it is also necessary to ferret the program out of management. To do that the designer should know what questions to ask. He needs to know, for instance, how many restaurants there are going to be, what type of food will be served in them, at what price range? If there is to be a coffee shop, he should know if the waitress will pick up the check, if there is to be a counter, what proportion of tables will seat two as against four or six. Sometimes, as in the case of Marriott, the planning office supplies the designer with a layout of the restaurants showing all the banquettes, bars, and so on, and the designer works within those parameters. The designer must also seek information regarding banqueting facilities—will they be used for business meetings and social events and, if so, what proportion of each. He needs to ask about the guest rooms—what proportion of them will be singles, suites, connecting rooms; whether the clientele will be mostly single men, two men to a room, couples, or a mixed proportion of each.

These are but a few of the details that a designer will need to know if he is to mold the spaces esthetically and functionally for the type of clientele the operator wants and for others as well since no hotel has an entirely circumscribed clientele. If the designer is not persistent in prying management for the answers he needs, he will end up producing sketch after sketch before he hits on what the client had in mind. Few operators, if any, can understand or evaluate a professional's time. The person who employs a designer wants to know that his office is efficient and busy but refuses to understand why he doesn't have all the time in the world for him.

Clients can pose a special problem for practitioners of interior design, it is something everyone thinks he can do. The architect's contribution is, therefore, not valued as much as in other technical areas where the client knows he doesn't know anything. As a consequence, the client is often less willing to take the advice of experts, and more easily swayed by his wife, his neighbor, his tennis partner. In straight architectural work, the client won't argue as much, waste so much of your time, frustrate you so much.

Warren Platner, FAIA

The bar in the Bristol Place in Toronto, Canada.

THE BUSINESS OF DESIGN

Running a design office is no more glamorous than running a steel mill. The same economics apply. In any creative organization there has to be some controlling influence. Those backroom people in the creative department have to be controlled by the front office people who are dealing with the client and with the day-to-day financial problems. This is becoming even more important as it becomes increasingly costly to run a business.

A client who is business oriented, moreover, will have more respect for a designer who is business minded. The average client is not too concerned with beautiful interiors. His real concern is with the interiors as a merchandizing and selling tool. I find the only way to stay in business is to know something about business. Roland Gallimore, AIA, believes that the special skills and attitudes required by interior designers are primarily in the area of business—knowing the furniture business and how to deal with its frustrations—rather than in design itself. Interior and furniture designers, he points out, have historically been spinoffs from architecture, and some of the most renowned architects have also been the most respected designers of interiors and furniture, such as Le Corbusier, Aalto, Mies, and Breuer. "The problem of delays in deliveries is something everyone has to live with," as Gallimore puts it. But if the interior designer is in at the beginning of a project, orders can be placed with delays in mind.

The one-person interior design business has little place in today's profession except in residential work. Too many disciplines are needed: too many kinds of expertise are required. A designer is forced to learn the language of engineers, of site planners, of acoustic and food consultants, and so on. There is so much specialization that the person who could

Cocktail lounge in the Colonnade in Boston.

comprehend the entire concept is on the way out. Tunnel vision is in. While the engineers and other technical members of the design team deal in formulas and BTUs, we deal in the intangibles—textures, lighting, people. Interior design involves all the necessary backup and paperwork, but it also involves that one element that makes the hotel special—the ambience. It is the only empirical discipline, and for that reason, everyone thinks he knows something about it.

Today's hotel designer then needs to be familiar with many disciplines. He needs to understand environmental problems and psychological problems. He needs to know about contracts and food service. He needs to keep abreast of new furniture and equipment and know how to purchase it. He needs to know that guest rooms are not necessarily the most profitable part of a hotel and that liquor makes money. He needs to know that young people are the affluent members of today's society, and therefore modern design is more appropriate than traditional. He needs to know that people expect certain standards. They expect Kleenex and good illumination in the bathroom. They expect wall-to-wall carpet, convenient closet space, and more often than not, two full-size beds in the bedroom. Today's hotel designer needs to know how to handle payrolls, how to deal with committees, and how to keep meeting reports. He has to know he is dealing with corporations that believe in paperwork. The legendary hotel tycoon of yesterday, such as Ellsworth Statler, Ernest Henderson, and Conrad Hilton, are a vanishing breed. Any personal relationship between the designer and management today is rare.

Let's face it, nobody but you cares much about your firm, but they do care about what your firm can do for them—what advantages they can derive from associating with it.

Habitation Leclerc, an exotic resort in Port-au-Prince, Haiti, consists of a cluster of villas on what was once the estate of Napoleon's sister, Pauline Bonaparte Leclerc. Each villa has a living room, bedroom, and a bath with access to a patio.

3. The Consultants

"The design profession has evolved from an art to almost a science," says Jordan Berman, authority on space planning. "Today, above all else what we achieve must function effectively. It makes sense to contact a specialist in lighting, acoustics, a dozen other specialties. Today's specialists have information on products that will be marketed three months from now."

This is especially true in the complex field of hotel design. Hotel architect William B. Tabler, who has designed some 400 hotels all over the world, says he doesn't believe in consultants being captives of the architect. "I want design judgment from them. I want a reaction."

As interior designers, we have been involved in projects with four or more consultants—all experts in their own field—in order to achieve a team capable of executing a commission. A lighting consultant can help enhance or change the mood of an interior; a graphics consultant can provide an image and inform the guest; a landscape architect creates the setting and advises on the interior planting; an acoustical consultant can provide the most effective level of sound. All of them aid and abet the work of the interior designer.

Consultants are usually paid a fee for a particular project—sometimes by the designer and sometimes by the client. If the fee is paid by the designer, it will be spelled out in the contract. But no matter who pays him, a consultant on the interiors, particularly a lighting consultant, should be responsible to the interior designer.

THE ROLE OF THE LIGHTING CONSULTANT

Lighting has been an important element of hotel design ever since 1882 when New York's old Hotel Everett "blazed forth with one hundred and one of Edison's incandescents in its main dining-room, lobby, reading-room, and parlors," and its use has become evermore sophisticated.

The drama and excitement of today's lighting is a comparatively recent development. Lighting consultant Leslie Wheel attributes it to the hung ceiling which came into existence after World War II as a result of air conditioning. Anything you did with light before that was visible. The hung ceiling made it possible to achieve effects that had previously been impossible.

Lighting must be considered as integral to the total design, not as an element imposed on other design elements. Again, as lighting consultant David A. Mintz puts it, "It is the art and the science working together, what the lighting designer can contribute. Well-planned, tasteful, unobtrusive lighting is not a mystery, but a complex series of small details. Lighting is only one of numerous disciplines to be considered by an interior designer. It is 100 percent the occupation of the lighting consultant."

Hotel lighting is a many-splendored thing. The lighting designer has to capture the mood and spirit of each space, whether it is a supper club or a meeting room, a bedroom or a banquet hall, an elevator or a coffee shop, a grand atrium space or an intimate cocktail lounge. In short he works with the interior designer to make the hotel fulfill its function—be it a big commercial hotel, a small elegant hotel, or a resort hotel. As

Virtually everyone involved in interiors cautions that few, if any, architects can hope just to walk into actual space planning and interior design and succeed unless armed with special training and/or experience. That would be like asking a vet to do heart surgery.

George Nelson, FAIA, FIDSA

The guest room doors at the Omni International in Atlanta are set in niches marked by overhead recessed lights so that the otherwise plainly finished hall is a pattern of light and shadow.

Above: Reception area and lobby in the Hyatt Regency in Manila, Philippines.

Right: The indoor pool at the Rye Town Hilton Inn in Rye, New York, was designed to suggest summerhouse treillage.

Above: Close-up of the ballroom lighting in the Inter-Continental London.

Left: The ballroom of the Inter-Continental London depends on changes of lighting to provide the right mood for a variety of functions.

lighting designer Howard Brandston says, "You can never make a person feel comfortable or secure unless he or she looks well and that is probably the main guiding principle of hotel lighting as well as hotel design."

THE ROLE OF THE GRAPHICS CONSULTANT

A hotel is often a microcosm of a city. In addition to retail and leisure activities, there are residential activities; there may be a heliport on top, a metro station below. Several floors of offices and several floors of condominium residences may be part of the hotel complex. There obviously has to be some way of directing people to where they want to go, and graphics in one form or another are the logical answer. Graphics are necessary, if for no other reason, to identify a hotel on the outside. But in a building with as many varied interior spaces as in a hotel, it is also necessary to have some kind of directional information inside. No hotel operator wants to keep the name of his hotel secret any more than he wants to conceal the way to a bar or restaurant. A confused guest is not a happy guest. Perhaps the exception that proves the rule is the new Berkeley in London which is so sure of its reputation that its name does not appear on the outside.

"The trouble is interiors are simplifying their esthetics at the same time they complicate their plans," as graphics designer John Follis states in the June 1976 *Interiors.* "A signage system to identify a project and control vehicular and pedestrian traffic outside, should be seen as a vital phase of the interior design program." And of course it is necessary that directional devices blend with the hotel's design.

Sometimes a hotel chain works directly with a graphics agency to create brochures and advertising material. In that case the agency graphics designer coordinates with the interior designer on all the hotel graphics. If the graphics designer is an independent consultant and graphics are part of the overall design, he should be in on the project at the beginning along with the other members of the design team. Follis points to several reasons, in addition to the fabrication budget, why this is desirable. Among them: "To ensure that power outlets and lighting fixtures are placed in optimum locations for interior signing needs . . . to coordinate signs with architectural elements, i.e., elevator call lights or variations in background colors and materials. Sign location is often critical, and early location is helpful in avoiding esthetic conflicts. . . ."

Interior designers do not generally include the design of a signage program as part of their fee, but if the system is to function and be esthetically related to the other elements of the interior, they should work closely with the graphics consultant. Restaurants, particularly, can rely heavily on graphics for their image.

THE ROLE OF THE LANDSCAPE ARCHITECT

The landscape architect might be the first member of the design team on the project since he is often responsible for the master planning of the entire area. This is particularly true in new urban and resort complexes in which various types of functions are incorporated—offices, shopping centers, hotels, theaters, and so on. A hotel is usually an important feature of such urban complexes, and it is invariably the center of the resort complex. To cite but one example, a 500-acre resort complex on the Babin Kuk peninsula in Yugoslavia recently planned by landscape architects and planners EDSA features nine hotels along with restaurants, a shopping center, an open-air theater, children's playgrounds, and a variety of sports facilities.

Landscape architects, moreover, are becoming more involved with the hotel interior since indoor planting has become an important part of the design, particularly in atriums. Thus the interior designer becomes involved with the landscape architect who specifies the indoor as well as outdoor planting. The interior designer, moreover, needs to know what plants will live in certain environments, something about overall atmos-

Opposite page from top to bottom:

Logo of the Arizona Biltmore in Phoenix.

Logo of the MGM Grand Hotel in Las Vegas, Nevada.

Symbol signs for the pool and coffee shop at the Crown Center Hotel in Kansas City, Missouri.

Logo for the Holiday Inn Mart Plaza in Chicago.

GRAPHICS PROGRAM

1. Basic image

Creation of symbol
Design of logo
Selection of alphabet to be used consistently throughout the hotel
Selection of colors

2. General hotel graphics

Architectural signs, sculptured/illuminated
Elevator button panel
Elevator cab posters, directory of public areas
Hotel Services directory, main lobby and each guest floor lobby
Interior and exterior traffic and directional signs
Interior Signs:
  Bell captain
  Cashier
  Door numbers
  Elevators
  Mailing information
  Reception
  Rest rooms
  Shop signs
  Travel and tour signs

3. Operating supplies

a. Advertising and promotion
Hotel and convention brochures
Postcards
Room tariffs
Sales kit folders
Tent cards
Welcome booklet

b. Bar supplies
Swizzle sticks

c. Guest supplies
Fire plan card
Garment bags, laundry and valet
Guest note pads
Guest pens
Guest soap wrappers
Guest stationery
Guest stationery folders, including information directory
Matches for each outlet
Sanitary disposal bags
Shoe cloths
Shower caps
Signs: Do Not Disturb/Make Up Room
Special suite stationery
Telephone directory covers
Travel bags

d. Laundry supplies
Laundry box
Polythene bags for valet
Shirt bags

e. Menus and wine list
Banquet menu covers and inserts
Coffee shop breakfast menu
Coffee shop menu
Door knob menu
Lobby bar drink list
Pool bar drink list
Pool bar menu
Room service menu and wine list (may also include hotel directory)
Specialty restaurant bar menu
Specialty restaurant wine list

f. Miscellaneous
Cloak room tag
Folders for presentation of guest checks
Guest room key tags
Hotel flags

g. Paper supply
Coasters for each outlet
Napkins

h. Printing and stationery
Calling cards
Labels
Office stationery: local, air mail, and memo

Accounts
Compliment slips
Credit card appplication
Credit card folder
Credit card guest check for various outlets
Guest folios
Safety deposit box record

Bell captain
Baggage claim check
Baggage sticker
Baggage tag

Front office
Group key envelopes
Guest questionnaire
Guest registration card
Hospitality (check-out) card
Message form and window envelope
Telegram form

Laundry
Laundry and dry cleaning list

i. Casino supplies
Cards
Chips
Dice
Layouts

Davenport's Famous Waffle Foundry

Louis M. Davenport came to Spokane in 1888 with exactly $1.25 in his pocket. Before long, his capital had increased to $125.00. Under a huge sign, proclaiming his new venture, he opened "Davenport's Famous Waffle Foundry." He bought a waffle iron and a tent and set up business on the corner of Post and Sprague.

A few months later, he bought a lot in the block across the street, where this hotel now stands. In 1914, with the cooperation of one hundred stockholders, the Davenport Hotel was built at a cost of three million dollars. Davenport's hospitable nature and his genius to do the unusual combined with his passion for beauty and an insistance of perfection of service, has brought the Hotel world fame.

Davenport's Famous Waffle Foundry's Breakfast

Cereals

With Milk	.55
With Cream	.65
With Sliced Banana	.75

An assortment of Crisp Dry Cereals, Oatmeal, and Cream of Wheat.

Fruits and Juices

Choice of Assorted Chilled Fruit Juices
Small — .55   Large — .75

Half Indian River Grapefruit	.55
Baked Washington Apple with Cream	.75
Stewed California Prunes or Kadota Figs	.65
Sliced Banana with Cream	.75
Iced Melon in Season	.75
Fresh Berries in Season	.75

Eggs and Omelettes

Single Egg, Any Style	.75
With Bacon, Link Sausage or Ham Steak	1.75
Two Eggs, Any Style	1.25
With Bacon, Link Sausage or Ham Steak	2.25

Three Egg Omelette
Western
filled with diced ham, onion, and green pepper...... 1.95
Jelly
filled with grape jelly.................... 1.95
Spanish
filled with a sauce of tomato, diced celery, onions and green pepper................... 1.95
Cheese
filled with melted American cheese.............. 1.95

Browned Corned Beef Hash and Egg............ 1.95

(The above orders served with hashed brown potatoes, buttered toast and preserves.)

Davenport's Mug of Hot Chocolate 35¢

Davenport's Egg Special

Two Country Fresh Eggs scrambled with Cream Cheese, Sherry and chives. Garnished with lettuce and tomatoes. Toast and jelly.
1.95

Davenport's Freshly Brewed Coffee 5¢ a cup

The Davenport Waffles

Old Fashioned Golden Waffles

Served with whipped butter and syrup or powdered sugar	.95
With preserves or cinnamon	.95
With Blueberries	1.50
With Strawberries	1.65

The Davenport
Served with two country fresh eggs 1.55

George Wafflington
With cherries and whipped cream 1.50

Johnny Apple-seed
With apples, cinnamon and whipped cream 1.50

Pretty Face
With half jumbo peach and whipped cream.......... 1.65

Louis D's Special
Topped with two scoops of ice cream, hot fudge, whipped cream, nuts and maraschino cherry 1.75

With Bacon, Ham Steak or Link Sausage
Extra 1.00

Pancakes and Breads

Buttermilk or Buckwheat Pancakes	.95
Silver Dollar Blueberry Pancakes (6)	1.25
Old Fashioned French Toast, powdered sugar	.95

With Bacon, Ham Steak or Link Sausage
Extra 1.00

Danish Pastry (2)	.55
Fresh Doughnut (2)	.55
Buttered Toast	.35
Toasted English Muffin	.40
Raisin or Cinnamon Toast	.45
Blueberry Muffin	.60

Club Breakfasts

Choice of assorted fruit juices, half Indian River grapefruit, stewed California prunes or Kadota figs.

With choice of:
1. Hot or Dry Cereal with Milk.................... 1.50
2. Two Eggs, any style 1.75
3. One egg any style with Bacon, Link Sausage or Ham Steak... 2.15
4. Golden Waffle with hot syrup and whipped butter............ 1.75

Hot buttered toast with preserves, coffee, pot of tea, or homogenized milk.

Beverages

Freshly Brewed Coffee	.05
Pot of Tea or Sanka	.30
Homogenized Milk	.30
Hot Chocolate	.35

Menu from the Davenport Hotel's Famous Waffle Foundry in Spokane, Washington.

pheric conditions, and automatic care for the plants, so that he can work with both landscape architect and lighting consultant in achieving the proper planting, positioning, and lighting of the indoor greenery. The contractor who puts the plants in place should also maintain them. Some hotels even maintain their own greenhouses.

THE ROLE OF THE FOOD SERVICE CONSULTANT

Since much of the food service in today's hotels is displayed in open kitchens and rotisseries, food service becomes part of the hotel's interior image. It is thus necessary for the interior designer to have an intimate knowledge of the role and activities of food consultants. Such equipment as oven hoods and cooking utensils can become as much a part of the design concept, in conjunction with the tableware and linens. The designer, moreover, must be aware of the relationship of back-of-the-house food services and restaurants, and their relationship with exits and entrances, where the bar service is located, and so on. He must understand food service as it applies to rooftop dining, coffee shops, and other hotel dining areas including convention facilities. All these areas are discussed in Chapter 5.

The pool with its surrounding terrace at the
Kah-Nee-Ta Lodge in Warm Springs, Oregon,
creates the impression of a small pond in a
mountain valley. The resort hotel is owned by the
Confederated Tribe of the Warm Springs
Reservation.

Opposite page top: A small lake within the inner court of Dublin's Airport Hotel was designed to be looked at rather than to use.

Opposite page bottom: Interior court at Skelligs Hotel in Dingle, County Kerry, Ireland.

Left: Omni International Atlanta is part of the Omni complex that includes at its core two 14-story office buildings, an entertainment center, ice skating rink, and a convention/meeting room center which connect with the hotel by a walkway. The view is looking toward the skating rink across the hotel's French Restaurant terrace. Guest room balconies are at left, office building at right.

Below: The French Restaurant Terrace in the Omni International Hotel in Atlanta.

4. Types of Hotels

There are urban hotels and resort hotels. There are suburban hotels and airport hotels. There are old prestige hotels and new prestige hotels. There are also motels. But over the years many of the original motels have tended to merge their characteristics of convenience with the amenities of hotels until there is little difference between them. A new generation of motel people, however, has sprung up who are returning the motel industry to its original concept: an inexpensive place to spend the night along the highway without all the frills of a hotel.

Airport hotels cater primarily to businesspeople who may fly in one night, spend the day conducting business in one of the hotel's meeting rooms, and fly out that night. Urban hotels, of course, may cater to business people, tourists, the affluent young, among others. But there is also the prestige hotel that caters to a genteel clientele who value service and privacy. It may be one of the older hotels such as the Plaza in New York or the Beverly Hills Hotel in Los Angeles. It may be one of the newer and more intimate hotels such as the Regency in New York or the refurbished Whitehall in Chicago. The latter was a dilapidated residential hotel with a fine private restaurant when we undertook the total restoration. It now boasts an excellent reputation as one of the ten best hotels in the country, according to *Fortune* magazine. A hotel is not better because it is new, but an old hotel has to keep its prestige intact. Once it has acquired a bad reputation, it is almost impossible to revive it.

In an urban hotel you are dealing mainly with interior environment. In a resort hotel you try to create stimulating environments, but not at the expense of the major environment which is the area or country in which the hotel is located. When you enter a resort hotel, you want to feel a relationship with the natural environment. You want to feel as the early American poetess Mrs. Sigournay did when she visited a hotel at Nahant on the New England coast in the middle of the 19th century: "It was built in 1820 of the native stone by which it is surrounded and contains a sufficient number of apartments for a multitude of guests. From the double piazza that engirdles it, is a succession of grand and extensive prospects, and a bracing ocean atmosphere. When long rains prevail, the mist enwraps it in a curtain, like a great ship in the midst of the sea." And that sense of place is what the designer of a modern resort hotel should try to achieve in spite of such counteracting 20th-century amenities as air conditioning.

The problem today, of course, is how to create that sense of place in a resort hotel that may be a reinforced concrete structure many stories high completely enclosed and without those engirdling piazzas. We worked on a hotel in Nassau—the Nassau Beach—where the problem was how to meld 20th-century techniques and such 20th-century amenities as a grand atrium space with the indigenous architecture of the island. Our solution was to use local artisans, native materials, native arts and artifacts, and native manufacturers to give the hotel an identity that makes it peculiar to that particular area. Sometimes, however, this sort of thing backfires. Hotel architect William B. Tabler tells of a hotel his firm designed in Central America for which the architects used a beautiful indi-

In the last 40 years the greatest influence on design has come from the concept of letting the esthetic grow out of the use of a structure rather than vice versa. The effect of this influence is a new, more objective, more natural esthetic. This applies to furnishings and interiors, as well as to architecture. Yet it is really not a new concept, but a greater acceptance of, and belief in, a concept proposed a much longer time ago.

Vincent Kling, AIA

The Hyatt Rio Mar in Rio Grande/Luquille, Puerto Rico.

genous glass mosaic in the bathrooms. "But the natives couldn't see why we didn't use tile. They thought we were making fun of them. We also used cement floor tiles hand done by native craftsmen but the natives would have preferred terrazzo."

In contrast we did a dramatic Hyatt Regency atrium hotel with architects Rader Mileto of Rome in a remote area of Namak Abroud on the Caspian Sea in which we intentionally ignored indigenous arts and crafts. Our reasons were that the hotel was designed for affluent Iranian tourists, most of whom live in Teheran and summer on the Caspian Sea, and that the Middle East has turned its back on local color and Asian craftsmanship in favor of the latest imports from the West. Thus the hotel furnishings as well as most of the construction materials came from the U.S. and Europe. The hotel is owned by a government-owned bank and is to be the focal point for a large resort complex that will be comprised of housing, highrise apartment blocks, a motor hotel, a marina, among other resort facilities. It took 5½ years to complete the hotel and the building costs were exorbitant. Nevertheless land values in the surrounding area have since increased tenfold, thus justifying the high costs.

In spite of the previous example, however, it is my opinion that a resort hotel should pay respect to its locale. Some hotel chains have such a strong identity you don't know if you're in Kansas City, London, Jamaica, or Miami. The guest in an urban hotel might pull back the blackout draperies and see a blank wall or a skyscraper across the street, but in a resort hotel it is the tenuous inside-outside relationship that is all important.

Often a resort hotel is in an isolated area and must fulfill all the needs of its guests—their food, entertainment, leisure activities—and that must be done in an exciting manner. Even a weekend guest can become bored. Thus you try to create stimulating environments but not at the expense of the natural environment outside. On the one hand, the walls should be minimized and the interiors opened up to the scenery. On the other hand, there should be a strong enough identity within the shell of the hotel to make it a special place and preferable to its competition. There also must be plenty of creature comforts inside the hotel to which guests want to return after a day on the tennis courts, the golf course, the ski slopes, the beach, or whatever, for a pleasant evening. If there is a nightclub it should not be like a nightclub you might find in downtown Des Moines, but a place with a resort flavor.

A CASE STUDY

This particular case study is intended to show how a hotel designed by one of the world's great architects can go wrong because of its interiors. The Hotel Nacional is situated west of Copacabana in Rio de Janeiro. It is a circular, 25-story structure designed by Oscar Neimeyer and built some 5 years ago in a resort area which is yet to be fully developed. Since it was constructed, however, a Sheraton and an Inter-Continental have gone up close by. Both the latter are conventional tourist hotels in design and layout. The Nacional, however, is unusual in that its public space was laid out with little thought for function. It happens that José Tjurs, a self-made man and operator of several hotel properties, paid Neimeyer only for his concept. Originally a cab driver in Rio, Tjurs made his fortune buying up bordellos that were no longer in use after World War II. Eventually he found himself in the hotel business, since bordellos with their many bathrooms make excellent hotels. Today, in his seventies, Tjurs owns eight major hotels in Brazil. A man who knows how to wheel and deal, he thought nothing of using someone as famous as Oscar Neimeyer to design his hotel for very little money and then finish it himself with a number of draftspeople, semi-architects, and engineers. As a result the Nacional is a striking piece of architecture on the outside, but inside it is a bouillabaisse. Without the services of an interior designer or help from

Unless a building is efficient, pleasant, and comfortable for the occupants, it doesn't work, no matter how well it may look to the person walking around it. Architecture cannot legitimately be separated from interior design.

Louis Beal

Top: Hotel Nacional-Rio in Rio de Janeiro, Brazil.

Bottom: Rio Inter-Continental in Rio de Janeiro, Brazil.

Neimeyer's office, it is an excellent example of how a hotel designed but not finished by an important architect can be a disaster. There is absolutely no coordination between the interiors and the architecture. It makes, in fact, an interesting comparison with the nearby Inter-Continental. One is an excellent piece of world architecture with little interior design; the other is a contemporary rubber stamp for which study and effort has been given to the interior design, backed up by experienced technical people who knew how to operate a hotel.

One feels that the Nacional is not sure of its market. While its personnel is oriented toward the Brazilian trade and the hotel has just under 500 rooms, they have added a major convention facility capable of handling some 2,000 people and are catering to travel agencies. In other words, they are courting an international trade that they are not equipped to handle, and yet they don't seem to be really orienting themselves in that direction. We spoke to local people who reacted favorably to the Inter-Continental and the Sheraton, both of which were executed by non-Brazilian interior designers. They seem to identify with them and would choose to go there rather than to their own flagship hotel designed by their own architect. Although these people are extremely nationalistic, good design apparently outsells nationalism.

Below: Suite in the Whitehall Hotel in Chicago.

Opposite page top: Hotel Inter-Continental in London.

Opposite page bottom: The Barbados Hilton.

Right: The Newport Beach Marriott in Newport Beach, California.

Below: Hotel Marina Palace in Helsinki, Finland.

Opposite page top: Loews Monte Carlo.

Opposite page bottom: The Alladin Hotel in Las Vegas, Nevada.

Omni International Atlanta.

Kah-Nee-Ta Resort Lodge on an Oregon Indian
reservation.

BALI HYATT IN BALI, INDONESIA

The Bali Hyatt is an example of a tourist hotel that takes its architectural and decorative cue from its locale.

Top: Exterior.

Middle: Exterior.

Bottom: Outdoor restaurant.

Opposite page top: Cocktail lounge.

Opposite page middle: Coffee shop.

Opposite page bottom: Suite.

5. Hotel Spaces and Their Function

"The Waldorf-Astoria ... is reduced to confessing ... across the traffic and the danger, how little, outside her mere swing-door, she can do for you. She seems to admit that the attempt to get at her may cost you your safety, but reminds you at the same time that any good American, and even any good inquiring stranger, is supposed willing to risk that boon for her. ' ... you must make a dash for it, but you'll see I'm worth it.' If such a claim as this be ever justified, it would indubitably be justified here; the survivor scrambling out of the current ... finds in the amplitude of the entertainment awaiting him an instant sense of applied restoratives...."

Such is the way the old Waldorf-Astoria struck Henry James in 1904, and such is the way any modern urban hotel keeper would like his hotel to beckon to today's passerby. The hotel entrance, of course, has much to do with whether it does or not.

Years ago a hotel man said to me that doors are to keep people out. The hotel entrance was a pompous affair designed as banks were designed to convey the impression of solidity and prestige. But the hotel entrance of today—whether it be a motel, a resort or city hotel, an airport or suburban hotel—should have what I call a nonexistent type of entrance. Of course doors are necessary as weather barriers, but a hotel entrance should be gracious. It should beckon the public in. If you drive into a garage and don't have to worry about the weather, there should not be any barrier between inside and outside.

The other extreme is an impressive entrance with magnificent bronze doors and a uniformed doorman to open them. The bronze door approach is not appropriate for a resort hotel or a convention hotel, but it might be the solution for a small, elegant urban hotel. It is really a matter of knowing the market: who is going to use the facility. Today, however, distinctions between different types of hotels are less easily defined than they once were. There is inevitably some overlap. Resort hotels cater to conventions and urban hotels cater to vacationers. Nevertheless once inside the door it should be immediately apparent what kind of hotel it is. If it is a resort hotel, for example, there might be a vista through the lobby to a swimming pool or planted area.

Because of tax laws, businesses that hold conventions in a resort hotel must have a legitimate convention and the hotel must have the facilities to support it, including the so-called ballroom or large meeting room, private meeting rooms, audiovisual equipment, and all the ancillary services required for a business convention. The hotel also needs facilities to entertain wives and children who may have come along for a vacation. Since most hotel operators accept business from everywhere—whether it is someone who wants a room for a night, a company that wants to hold a shareholder's meeting, a father who wants his daughter married in the grand ballroom—it is up to the design team to make the hotel flexible enough to handle all these functions and more.

In the realm of attitudes, for instance, one must deal with the fact that although the exterior of a building, once completed, is generally fixed almost forever, its interior is something that people not only work and live in, but work on. In order to effectively plan interior spaces, changed patterns of use must be anticipated, which allow for alterations in company policy and personnel preferences. "Our work is cast not in concrete, but in cotton."

Norman DeHaan, AIA

A double room in the Hotel Marina Palace in Helsinki, Finland.

Opposite page top left: Entrance to Bristol Place, a business and meeting hotel near the Toronto airport.

Opposite page top right: Covered entrance shelters clusters of four rooms at the Hammamet Sheraton, a resort hotel near Tunis in an area with a rich Arab background.

Opposite page bottom: Main entrance to the Alladin Hotel, a resort/convention hotel on Las Vegas's strip.

Above: Contemporary Resort-Hotel at Disney World, Florida, features a monorail about to enter the hotel through an air curtain end wall.

Left: Disney World's Contemporary Resort-Hotel in Florida features the so-called Grand Canyon Concourse, containing restaurants, shops, indoor monorail station, and a 9-story ceramic tile mural.

57

RECEPTION AREAS/LOBBIES

The reception area, comprised of lobby, reception desk, elevator foyers, baggage handling, and so on, is a multipurpose area. It is the first impression that a guest has of the interior of the hotel and it should welcome rather than overwhelm. If it does the latter, the guest may think that the room rates are higher than he expected.

John Portman, designer of the pioneering Hyatt Regency, has shown in his design of subsequent hotels that the problem of the Atlanta atrium can be overcome. In the Hyatt Regency in Chicago, for instance, the guest normally arrives at the automobile entrance. From here he is whisked to the reception desk where he registers. Then, after he has gone through the nitty-gritty of the mechanical functions and is a guest of the hotel, he goes up an escalator and the fantastic atrium space explodes on him.

The hotel experts predicted that the Atlanta Hyatt Regency would be a failure. And from an operational standpoint it probably is less of a success than a hotel that is designed by a hotel operator to function in a logical fashion. But it makes up for its lack of efficiency with the excitement of its architecture. It has become a landmark and is generating revenue from a great many people who come to admire the architecture, stay to have a drink or a cup of coffee, and go away to recommend the hotel to friends. Thus it is only negative from a hotelier's point of view. From a design or architectural point of view it is an exciting, positive place.

It stands to reason that when you carve a huge hole out of a structure to create such a magnificent space, the logistics have to suffer. In terms of room service, it is a problem to keep food hot. Having to move guests and luggage and service carts such distances is hard on carpets as well as personnel. However, it is a place where people can congregate. It is the grand plaza that most American cities lack. Its importance in those terms cannot be overemphasized even if it is achieved at the cost of the intimacy and friendliness of the small lobby, which is something that everyone can relate to. "This is my club." "This is my hotel." "This is where I sit and read the *Wall Street Journal, London Times, Le Martin....*"

There is a certain surrealism about the atrium lobby that makes it a stimulating experience. It's like a little garlic. It's a wonderful spice if you use it properly, but if it is overdone, it can ruin everything else.

The Atlanta Hyatt Regency was the pioneer as far as the jet-age atrium hotel is concerned, but it has its precedents. Denver's 19-century Brown Palace, which is still going strong, has a central atrium with balconies as corridors for rooms, and San Francisco's Palace Hotel completed in 1875 had a "grand central court" with its crystal-roofed garden filled with rare and exotic plants, statuary, and fountains. It was only logical to recapture the idea and give it a new look.

Since Portman revived the atrium idea, a new generation of atrium hotels has been devised as a collaboration between an operator and an architect in which the atrium is still an integral part of the building and yet removed from the traffic flow and material flow of hotel operation. The Hyatt Regency in Montreal is the result of collaboration between the architect, hotel planner, and operator. It incorporates the exciting space without interfering with the normal function of the hotel.

We collaborated on an atrium lobby for the Myrtle Beach Hilton in South Carolina with architect W. Crutcher Ross, which was an attempt at grandeur within a limited budget and without the usual fabulous glass elevators. To create drama we used a monumental tapestry—75 ft (23 m) long and 12 ft (3.6 m) wide—which hangs on the elevator core and carries the eye up through the atrium—a function usually accomplished by the kinetic activity of the glass elevators. The tapestry was executed in Germany from our design in a combination of hand and machine techniques. Our lighting consultant worked with us to give it maximum impact. It

Rather than an atrium, the lobby of the Hyatt Regency Chicago is a three-level conservatory featuring a rain curtain/waterfall and sculpture. A cafe extends from one corner of the lobby into an adjoining conservatory.

The lobby of the newly renovated Whitehall in Chicago.

brings striking color to an otherwise neutral shell of spartan white stucco.

There are some hotels, of course, for which the spatial excitement of an atrium is not appropriate. The Inn on the Park in London, for instance, is dignified, pleasant, and elegant, but it has none of such American gadgetry as glass-enclosed elevators, sparkling lights, waterfalls, and fountains. The Whitehall in Chicago, for which we teamed up with architect Raymond Giedraitis, has a miniscule lobby. It is operated by Lex Hotels, Ltd., an English-based company which wanted to attract an affluent, sedate clientele—those more interested in service than grandeur. We created an intimate clublike atmosphere in the lobby, using modern versions of the overstuffed chair, rich materials—leather, glass, brass, and marble—all within the context of what most people consider contemporary design. We try to design according to that definition, but we also think ahead. If an investment is made in good furnishings, we don't want to do something that will have to be completely changed a few years later because it is out of date. The best approach to avoiding that kind of obsolescence is to take a long, hard look backward to see what has withstood the test of time, to resist trends, and yet to try to go beyond what is being done today. It may be risky to decide what will be done 5 or 10 years hence, but if you have a team of people who have proven themselves in terms of taste, you can generally extrapolate what will be from what has been.

Today's hotel lobby can be a grandiose volume or an intimate space. Both are valid. The huge atrium lobby is an adventurous experience. It is the grand spectacle superseding old-world hotelier traditions, while the small lobby gives an opposite impression of personalized service.

More and more designers are becoming aware that they are not designing for other designers or for posterity. They are designing for the comfort of people and insofar as they accomplish that the operator will get a return on his investment. That is what hotel design is all about. People don't really appreciate a hotel as an architectural statement, especially in an urban setting where it is surrounded by other big buildings. All they see is a canopy and doors. And what happens beyond those doors is the realm of the interior designer, interior architect, design consultants, the lighting and graphic specialists—the whole design team. We form a team of experts who depend on one another to achieve a concept and then set about in the most logical way to have it executed within the parameters of the budget.

The reception area in today's hotel is also the lounge or the lobby. These spaces are increasingly less defined by partitions or even changes in floor materials. It is all one space. So the registration area can be part of the space where you might have a cocktail, wait for a cab, check your luggage. And that space must be designed to accommodate all these functions. People rarely sit in a lobby and watch other people as they once did. If a large sofa happens to be in the center of the area, no one will sit on it. It is too exposed. People like to sit in small, comprehensible groups.

Hotel operators and designers alike are realizing that large atrium spaces can be dehumanizing to sit in, and they have tried various ways of counteracting this. In many of the big atrium lobbies, for instance, there are bars which not only create a merchandising function in the area but provide people with a place to cluster. Some have portable bars (modified electric golf carts) so that a hostess can bring a drink to a guest sitting in a lounge chair. Various kinds of canopies have been devised to create a cocktail lounge within the larger space. The lighting designer plays an important role in bringing a human scale to atrium spaces through subtle variations of light. "You have to think of it in terms of its distinct areas—planting, fountains, seating groups," according to Howard·Brandston, and light each accordingly. To do this, he explains, "We select lamps with a special focus pattern and range so that no matter at what distance we mount them, we can control the various areas to be lit."

These more humanized spaces are the result of design team collaboration. A growing respect is being generated among good architects and good designers for the contribution each can make toward achieving good architecture. And by good architecture I mean everything from the structural engineering of the building right down to the selection of ashtrays. It's all architecture.

I don't believe any significant statement has ever been achieved as the result of an architect creating a shell and then a designer taking over and superficially decorating the space. The best test is time. A hotel can't afford to be a current fad as a restaurant sometimes is. A hotel represents an investment of many dollars.

After all, the reason for carving out space is to let people function comfortably within it. What the architect, the operator, the designer want to achieve is a successful merchandising statement. That is what a successful hotel must be. There are few buildings more intimately entwined with merchandising, with the possible exception of shopping cen-

We've always had an interior design division. To my mind, there is no such thing as interior architecture and exterior architecture—they're one and the same thing. What happens inside determines what happens outside, and if you don't have this in mind while you're designing a building, you can get some pretty brittle results.

Vincent G. Kling, AIA

Lobby of the Algonquin Hotel, one of New York's famous landmark hotels.

Opposite page top: More residential in feeling than Atlanta's other new hotels, the Omni International caters mainly to corporate and holiday travelers.

Opposite page bottom: Lounge area in the Hotel Marina Palace in Helsinki, Finland.

ters. Cathedrals were built to give people a spiritual awareness, but a high hotel ceiling is meaningless unless it makes the cash register ring.

As for the future, I think as a result of the interaction among architect, designer, and operator, the hotel lobby will become physically smaller but certainly no less dramatic an environment. Aside from a few airline terminals or athletic stadiums, the most exciting expression of interior spatial volume is in hotels. No one is building magnificent edifices for the railroads anymore, and airline terminals are usually miserable places to be in. The hotel lobby is the most exciting space to be found in many cities around the world because it is probably the grandest space and more thought has been given to human comfort within it.

A great many hotel operators, designers, and architects are realizing that a hotel can no longer be just a hotel in the purest sense. It is a number of things—an entertainment center, a convention center, a merchandising center, a place to rendezvous, a landmark. It is almost anything except just a place to put your bags down and go to bed. The idea of shops in a hotel is also part of the hotel image but it is a double-edged sword. While shops present a chance for dignified merchandising activity and can enhance the reputation of the hotel, they can work the other way if not carefully integrated into the total design.

Top: The Gazebo Lounge of the Rye Town Hilton Inn in Rye, New York, was designed like the rest of the inn to look as if it were a country house.

Middle: Lounge at the Bristol Place, which is near the Toronto airport.

Bottom: Lobby of the Sheraton Atlanta.

Opposite page: Lounge of the Kah-Nee-Ta Resort Lounge in Warm Springs, Oregon, a resort hotel owned by the Confederated Tribe of the Warm Springs Reservation.

Right: The sunken foyer lounge with marble flooring and high-backed seating units is the main feature of the public areas in the Airport Hotel in Dublin. The ceiling in this one-story area is rough timber diagonal sheeting with clusters of square roof lights.

Below: The lounge of the Skelligs Hotel in Dingle, County Kerry, Ireland, is as homelike as the exterior. A tourist hotel, it is comprised of a series of small buildings in scale with its scenic locale.

THE RECEPTION DESK

Electronic data processing, preregistration, and reservation services could render the traditional reception desk obsolete, but I don't think it would be practical to eliminate it. We have been involved with hotels where the front desk has been replaced by a table at which the assistant manager or receptionist sits the guest to sign the check-in form. This procedure is feasible for a small hotel, such as the Georges V in Paris where it works successfully, but in a large property of 500 rooms or more it would be difficult to completely eliminate the reception desk. There are, of course, various devices for preregistering guests—on the plane or bus en route from the airport or even at the airport.

Today's major hotels have computers that operate, at the least, the air conditioning and alarm system. These computers have the capacity to accommodate many more systems, and they might be able to register a guest in his room. It would, however, be disconcerting to have people wandering around the corridors if they are not yet registered. People have to "belong." Everybody takes his paranoia with him when he packs his bags. People tend to lose their identity in a strange place, and an important part of hotel design is to make them feel secure. When I am in my hotel room and lock the door, I want to feel that no one is going to disturb my privacy.

It seems to me that the concierge system could be incorporated into more American hotels. The cashier system, too, needs rethinking. There should be quicker ways to check out, especially during heavy periods. A guest is usually in a hurry to check out and there should be a design solution to facilitate this.

Baggage handling is another problem. It seems to me the best proce-

Reception area in the Jerusalem Hilton.

dure would be to take the luggage from the guest and put it on conveyors. After the guest has checked in, the luggage would be received in his room. This would alleviate the usual method of the doorman picking up the bags and stacking them in an unsightly heap in the lobby. The reason this system has not been generally adopted is because some think that it might make a guest feel uneasy to surrender his luggage at the door. However, the airlines do it, and everyone takes it for granted. And although airlines sometimes lose luggage, losing a bag in a hotel is not as probable as having a bag go to another geographical destination.

ELEVATORS AND ELEVATOR FOYERS

An elevator foyer might be off the lobby or within it, but wherever it is and no matter the number of elevators, people will have to stand and wait for them with little to do but contemplate the elevator doors, the twinkling lights, or other people. The designer should keep this in mind as well as the wear and tear that the foyer will inevitably receive. Whenever people have to stand they fidget, lean on walls, grind their feet into carpets. Elevator foyers, therefore, are difficult areas to make attractive. We have experimented with kinetic displays that exploit the elevator's own light system, but in a major hotel with many elevators, the cost of such displays can be prohibitive.

The interior of the elevator is also a problem for the designer. It is a confined environment and because of the abuse that all elevator surfaces receive and because today's elevators are uncontrolled spaces subject to vandalism, the selection of materials is important. The elevator may also be the guest's first introduction to the hotel if that is the method by which he enters it from his automobile. The surface materials, therefore, have to be sturdy as well as have vandal-resistant qualities, but such materials are generally not particularly attractive. We have found that a carpeted

Opposite page top: Reception desk at the Hotel Marina Palace in Helsinki, Finland.

Opposite page bottom: Reception area in the Zanadu Yacht & Tennis Club in Freeport, Grand Bahamas.

Below: Elevators in the Plaza's 59th Street lobby in New York. The Plaza was recently refurbished after it was taken over by Western International Hotels in 1974.

floor is preferable to a hard one because it serves as a mat to get rid of debris on people's feet. An elevator carpet, moreover, can more easily be replaced than the carpet immediately outside the elevator. The acoustical quality of carpet is also an asset. In fact we have used carpets on elevator walls as well as floors and found them not only abrasive resistant but acoustically valuable and comfortable. Carpeting is particularly suitable if one elevator wall is of glass for a panoramic view. In hotels wth such elevators, however, there has to be an alternative because some people have a fear of riding in them.

No standard size for elevators exists, but there is a standard cost for a building in terms of square feet, so elevators tend to be about the same size. Nevertheless we have worked on a project with three elevators of one size and three of another because the architecture of the building dictated an oddly shaped elevator shaft and thus the cars within it had to be of an odd dimension. But usually when the designer creates an unorthodox shape or size elevator, the cost begins to escalate disproportionately. This, however, may be justified if the elevators are a special feature of the hotel.

The number of elevators a hotel should have depends on the physical layout, the size of the hotel, and other factors. If there are public areas on upper floors, obviously more elevators are needed. If the public areas are all on the ground floor, fewer elevators are required. This is a problem that has to be figured out by the designers, elevator consultants, and the hotel operator.

BALLROOMS OR CONVENTION CENTERS

What is a ballroom today? Is it still a valid use of space, and if not, how can the space be justified? From a design standpoint, what should a ballroom be?

I don't know why we continue to label these spaces ballrooms. They are designed for large meetings, conventions, banquets, seminars, and almost anything except balls. Gone are the days when hotels competed for the social patronage of the elite who gave spectacular cotillions in their ballrooms. If the area is used for a ball today, it is usually a comparatively small affair for which movable partitions are used to subdivide the space.

Today's convention space then has to be divisable and totally self-sufficient. It should include its own entrance and be devoid of windows—an integrated internal space which is as flexible as possible. The term "convention center" seems to be a more appropriate name. It is an important part of a city hotel, not only for conventions but for a variety of community activities. It is also important in resort hotels because it can generate business during the off seasons. For tax purposes a business trip has to be a legitimate business trip, and if a resort hotel can supply the necessary facilities, it can capitalize on the additional convention market. There are many such hotels in resort areas. The Sheraton at Dubai on the Arabian Gulf, for example, has complete convention facilities, including such highly advanced technological necessities as audiovisual equipment, the potential for closed circuit television and for data handling via long-distance telephone, spaces in which to handle meeting registration, sufficiently large doorways to move exhibits in and out, entrances designed to handle convention traffic away from normal guest entrances, and so on. Meeting and convention facilities are also an important part of airport hotels as exemplified by the Lex-Heathrow Hotel in London which has a complete theater/seminar facility incorporating the most sophisticated audiovisual equipment.

Movable wall partitions make it possible to have a social function in one area of these large meeting rooms, a business meeting in another, and a seminar in still another. Today's movable wall systems are acoustically as good or better than permanent walls. Two types of systems are in general use: those that slide on tracks and others that are totally porta-

Interior decoration without design is merely employing a sense of colour, a knowledge of furniture and its arrangement, and the ability to select the appropriate accessories. Interior decoration with design is the art of professionally advising clients on creating a truly suitable interior, using a discerning and disciplined eye in order to reflect character and personality in the contemporary idiom, ensuring that all fit into the best of modern interior design.

David Hicks

Top: The ballroom in the new wing of the Beverly Wilshire in Beverly Hills, California.

Left: The banquet area in the Jerusalem Hilton is set up with round tables seating eight.

Above: The ballroom in the Hotel Borobudur Inter-Continental in Jakarta, Indonesia, is set up for a banquet.

ble and incorporate pneumatic parts so that air pressure balloons them into place and keeps them stationary until they are deflated and moved. Although the cost may be initially more than a builtin system, the engineered solution provides the hotel operator with a flexibility that enables him to realize a return on his investment far exceeding the one he would receive on a nonflexible space. Whereas a built wall is part of the original capital investment, and a movable partition is considered furniture and is thus amortized at a different rate, economic factors come into play which the designer should be aware of so that he can justify his solution and assist the operator in making the most use of the facility.

Since the convention center is usually an interior space, it is often through lighting more than anything else that the proper ambience can be achieved for a wedding, a business meeting, or a ball. The designer should spend a lot of time and effort to integrate lighting with an architectural solution to create spaces that are flexible. Lighting—its intensity and color—is an important factor in this. So-called white light might be used for a business meeting with sufficient brightness to read papers and make notes. A dim, soft pink light might be used to create an intimate atmosphere. Another method of transforming one of these interior spaces is by changing the ceiling height. If, for instance, there are not many people in a space, it might be advantageous to have a lower ceiling, which would not only make the space seem less alien but change the proportion of the walls. What seemed to be a square wall at the original ceiling height becomes a horizontal wall at a lower ceiling height. If, however, an auditorium is being used for projection purposes, the ceiling needs to be high to maintain proper sight lines above the heads of the viewers.

Because there is nothing to work with but ceiling, walls, and floor, it is a challenge to achieve the effect that is desired for a particular function in these interior spaces, whether it be a banquet, a seminar, a meeting, or a film showing. We are constantly searching for new materials and new techniques to deal with this problem.

FURNISHINGS FOR BANQUET FACILITIES

Should banquet tables be round or rectangular? Logic dictates that round tables which seat eight people are preferable for several reasons. A round table of a certain dimension seats eight comfortably while making it possible for each one to reach the middle of the table and to converse with everyone else without shouting. Eight people are probably the maximum number who can carry on an intelligible conversation together. A round table, too, is obviously the most democratic since it has no head and no foot. At a long rectangular table you can only talk to your neighbors. Long tables are a more institutional approach both esthetically and psychologically. Nevertheless they do provide maximum seating.

Although we would prefer to specify armchairs, they are just not feasible. It is necessary to have armless chairs in such multipurpose rooms so they can be stacked. An armchair is also wider than a side chair, and to increase the seating capacity the chair must be underscaled. Snap-on arms have been experimented with but such mechanisms rarely work in institutional design. Anything that swivels or is detachable is impractical because it breaks or is detached or stolen. It is a test of the public versus the product and inevitably the public wins. Even if it is a public that intends no malicious mischief, there is the occasional 250-pound man who sits down—and something has to give.

PREFUNCTION AREAS

The prefunction area is adjacent to the larger space where a meeting or some other event takes place. It might be a room in which people register, have a drink, meet their friends. It is, in fact, a comprehensible space next to the less comprehensible large area where personal contacts are difficult. Because designers have done their utmost to free these large

Even on our earliest jobs—back when we opened our office in 1966—we tried to make sure interior design was given the same careful consideration as other aspects of our projects. We tended to attract clients who were in sympathy with this approach and we began getting separate interior design commissions early on.

Stanley Daniels, AIA

We don't believe in specialization. The design staff is comprised entirely of architects, since everybody who works here must be able to work on everything. Architects who do interior design require specialized training—architectural schools have no curriculae in interiors. They graduate people who have no familiarity with the subject.

Warren Platner, FAIA

convention spaces of columns, people have nothing to migrate to but the peripheral wall. Thus the prefunction area provides a more human space in which to congregate. It also serves as a place in which to organize those attending the function away from the mainstream of normal hotel traffic. The prefunction area, therefore, should be designed as a flexible space that, like the inner meeting rooms, can change its character according to need.

PRIVATE MEETING ROOMS

Private meeting rooms are part of the convention complex. A private meeting room is just what its name implies: a comparatively small space in which groups of from 6 to 40 people can congregate for a meeting or where a businessman might entertain ten colleagues for lunch. Private meeting rooms are situated near the major meeting space so that they can be easily served from the banquet kitchen or room service kitchen. In a highrise building, the kitchen services and public spaces will probably be located in the lower portion of the building because that is where the building usually resolves into more of a horizontal expression. The upper verticality only provides space for guest rooms, corridors, elevators, and fire stairs; and a panorama lounge or restaurant might cap the whole thing. Such a configuration could be called the hotel cliche of the 1960s and 1970s. Logistically it is simpler to have the kitchen on the lower levels because of food delivery, garbage disposal, and so on. The convention complex, therefore, sometimes winds up being below street level, which presents a structural engineering problem to achieve such vast cavernous spaces without columns.

SEPARATE GUEST ENTRANCE

There should be separate entrances for regular hotel guests and for those who are attending a restaurant, a supper club, or a convention. There are several reasons for this, but the major one is the traffic problem. Sometimes the peak periods of check-in coincide with the arrival of guests for a social or business function. Or a person may arrive the night before a business meeting at the same time guests are arriving for a reception. Besides creating traffic problems such situations throw people together who have different objectives. The businessperson, for instance, may feel swept up in a crowd of party-goers.

Most major hotel projects being planned today take this into consideration and a lot of attention is given to positioning the property on the site so that people will go to the right entrance. Since the major incoming traffic in an urban hotel is by car, bus, or taxi, effort should be given to directing it to the proper entrance through landscape, architectural, and graphic design. Unfortunately at the Atlanta Hyatt Regency the social traffic (those going in to drink, dine, or attend a show) use the back door. That was probably not intended but happened because the city changed two-way streets to one-way streets after the building was up. But whatever the reason, the social traffic is continually making a mistake.

The ideal way to design a hotel would be to make a mock-up of it, see how people use it, and change it accordingly. Unfortunately the cost would be prohibitive. We can do this with certain areas, such as guest rooms, but not an entire hotel.

DINING ROOMS

In the 19th century the great test of the American hotel was its table. In 1854 an Englishman raved about the luxuries of the Mount Vernon Hotel in Cape May, especially its dining hall which, he tells us, was 525 ft (190 m) long and 60 ft (18 m) wide and "took first rank in size. Three thousand diners could be seated in it." The Grand Union in Saratoga, New York, had dinner menus which listed 50 dishes. And there was great consternation when the aristocratic old New York Hotel gave up the American plan to specialize in room service.

In the 20th century, however, necessity and inclination joined forces to keep Americans from indulging their appetites so extensively and hotel dining rooms went out of fashion. Now dining rooms are being revived as an important part of hotel design since they are not only a convenience to the guest but also a source of revenue for the management.

The new dining room, though, does not have the benefit of the many waiters and chefs that made those 50-dish menus possible. Staffing and rising costs are the main deterrents. So the solution has been to specialize. Steak rooms were among the first such restaurants to become popular in U.S. hotels. We pioneered the Rib Room which specializes in a limited menu—chops, steaks, roast beef, and maybe one or two other dishes. The original Rib Room color scheme—red, black, and barn wood—has, in fact, become a restaurant cliche. The advantage of such rooms is that the food can be served directly from the open-hearth or display kitchen which not only makes for easy service but minimizes the personnel necessary to run the kitchen. It also eliminates elaborate menus. Open-hearth cooking is a relatively recent phenomenon in hotel dining, but I think it is here to stay. It does, of course, place a severe restriction on the diversity of dishes and it places strong design parameters on the designer. The interior architecture and the mechanical systems have to take into account the open-hearth function.

"The validity of the display kitchen," as Peter Tishman, Food and Beverage Director for Sheraton Hotels in Europe and the Middle East, puts it, "is to bring cooking as close as possible to the service point." A display kitchen, he explains, "should not be an addition to a kitchen which has to operate in the back of the house because this is too expensive as far as the staff is concerned. The display kitchen should be self-sufficient . . . and the focal point of the room." He particularly cites the Movenpick in Munich as having an attractive restaurant area of this type. It is a large room with several areas specializing in different types of food—seafood in one area, special cold dishes in another, and fast service in another. Tishman sees this as a good solution for hotels of the future.

We asked several hotel people how they thought hotel restaurants could compete with outside establishments. "Apparently," Tishman replied, "people don't believe in hotel restaurants. If you had the same restaurant outside a hotel and in a hotel, the outside one would have more customers." He thought the only way to get around that would be for the hotel restaurant to have an outside entrance and, if possible, make it look as if it were not part of the hotel. He pointed out that there are many good examples of this in Germany, such as the Steidenberger Abbott Hotel where one restaurant called the Schweinsteiger is part of the hotel as far as the back of the house is concerned, but from the outside it seems to be completely free standing and separate.

John Andrews, independent Food and Beverage Consultant in Athens, also thought that creating the feeling of an independent restaurant was the solution. He believed, however, that the restaurant should have separate management. Trader Vic's is an example of this. It has placed its own special type of food merchandising into hotels, mainly Hiltons, with great success.

R. F. Hargreaves, a director of the Savoy Group in London, thought a hotel restaurant ought to do just as well as an outside restaurant if it offers the same or better food and service and is better from a decorative point of view.

But Sir Charles Forte, chairman of the board of the Trust House/ Forte group, believed that the success of a hotel restaurant depended on the country it is in. In Britain, he said, "many guests of a hotel eat in a hotel restaurant. In France the opposite is true. People stay in a hotel and eat outside and people outside come into the hotel to eat." Nevertheless Sir Charles believes the best way for a hotel restaurant to compete

Many architects think they can still approach interior work as though nothing has changed since the days when Herman Miller and Knoll furniture was used everywhere; it is ironic that architects who otherwise bristle at using predesigned building components are willing to do precisely that when it comes to interior work.

Norman De Haan, AIA, ASID

Left: The Rib Room, the original specialty restaurant designed by Henry End Associates, in the Heathrow Hotel at London's Heathrow Airport.

Below: Dining room in London's Howard Hotel, a modern hotel with old-world elegance.

with outside establishments is "in the usual way by giving first class food, good value, good service, and acquiring a reputation for good food." He also believed hotel restaurant business could "be inspired within the hotel if it is properly set up by the management, advertised in the elevators and guest rooms—and generally made a feature of."

After all, hotels should be places to dine just as they are centers of activity and entertainment. When checking into a hotel, one of the first things people say is, "Where shall we eat?" Hotel restaurants, therefore, should be visible, inviting, entertaining, and provide an ambience that makes dining a special occasion.

Not only are hotel restaurants and dining rooms a source of revenue and a way of keeping the guest within the physical confines of the hotel, but if they are good they will bring people back. Although many people say they want to go out and explore a new city when they get to the hotel, they often don't feel like venturing too far from it. And there are people too tired or too lazy to go out. Nowadays no one thinks anything of jumping on a plane in Frankfurt, going to a meeting in Milan, having dinner in London, and being in Frankfurt again next day; or jumping on a plane in Miami, attending a meeting in New York, going to Montreal, and then to San Francisco two days later. It is a jet world and people are using travel as a tool rather than as a luxury. These seasoned travelers can't afford to waste time, but they know what service is and they know what food is. They are on an expense account and could probably check into any hotel they want to, so why do they choose this one and why will they come back? The dining room can be one important reason. A hotel can also capitalize on the timid or lazy guests if they feel comfortable in their dining facilities.

Right: Dining room in the Hotel Villa Magna in Madrid, Spain.

Opposite page top: The sophisticated Cirque Restaurant in New York's Mayfair House.

Opposite page bottom: Henry VIII Restaurant in Holiday Inn Swiss Cottage in London.

Opposite page top: Kiawah Inn dining room in Atlanta.

Opposite page bottom: The Bugatti Restaurant in the Omni International Hotel in Atlanta is on the lobby floor and is illuminated by an open skylight.

Above: The French Restaurant in the Omni International Hotel in Atlanta.

Top: The Penthouse Restaurant with views of Old Plymouth, England, in the Holiday Inn Plymouth.

Bottom: Interior pool at the Hotel Marina Palace in Helsinki, Finland.

ROOFTOP FACILITIES

Rooftop dining is popular because of the rotating panorama lounge. Until recently the rooftop area was primarily a lounge with a bar where a guest would sit and sip a drink until he went full circle. To keep guests there longer, operators introduced food to stimulate more drinking as well as to make use of the space during the daytime.

Because of the difficulties of getting guests to and from a rooftop and because of the necessity of providing its own kitchen, I think rooftop facilities are only feasible in a few cases. First, there has to be a view and the hotel has to be high enough to justify it. But, as Hugo Garin, president of Amipex, an international food service company, puts it, "People usually only go up there once to see the view and if you don't have the right type of operation you never see those customers again." And, he adds, "It's more expensive to run the restaurant." Nevertheless rooftop facilities are still being built, so they are obviously a source of revenue.

What should the designer think about when working on a rooftop restaurant? The most important thing, of course, is not to impede the view. Designers sometimes forget that to see out there has to be more light outside the glass than in; therefore the room itself must be dimly lit. Nothing should reflect from the glass, such as the flame of a candle or any brightly lit object in the room. Although there is glass that has been chemically treated or abraded in such a way as to break up reflections, it also obscures the view. So it is essential to design the lighting and light levels with great care. In order to deal with angles of refraction you might have to tilt the windows, and although that is, or should be, an architectural problem, it is surprising how many architects are more concerned with the form of the building from the outside than they are with how it functions inside. The designer is continually having to remind the architect to recognize that whatever is done on the outside of a wall or window will affect the wall and the window on the inside.

Sometimes it will be necessary for the designer of a rooftop facility to create a view. For instance, an ocean panorama may look magnificent in the daytime but at night it becomes a black void. In that event the solution might be to make use of the glass as a mirror. This is accomplished by placing source light so that it will reflect. The image appears to be the same distance outside the plane of glass that it is from the glass on the inside. It might also be possible to create a "barbershop effect" by placing a mirror on the back wall that will reflect the interior lights that are reflected against the window glass. In this way you will have created an interior space that will revert to being a panorama space in the daytime when the lights are off.

Whether it is a rooftop restaurant or a dining area on the ground floor that is glass on all sides or three sides, light is a problem and so is color. Many architects want daylight, including skylights and clerestories. But once daylight enters a room, you have a completely uncontrolled situation as far as drama is concerned. The most successfully dramatic rooms are interior spaces.

A pavilion is a sort of denial of interior space. In a pavilion the outside becomes part of the inside. If there is a pavement outside the glass, it should continue into the room. If the outside of the building is white stucco, the ceiling should be white stucco so that the glass is simply an invisible curtain to keep the elements out and the pavilion appears to be part of the outside.

A rooftop space, however, is primarily a nighttime experience, and therefore color can be used because the lighting is subdued. In fact colors that might appear unattractive in daylight can become elegant in the kind of ambient light that is available from dusk on. If the room is also to be used in the daytime, it is a matter of where the color goes. For example, we have designed a rooftop food and beverage facility which is on two levels. The elevator lets guests off on the lower level, which is a cocktail

lounge and dance floor, and then they walk up to the rotating rooftop lounge and restaurant. The carpet in both facilities is charcoal-black. The color is repeated on the upholstery so that when the space is empty, there appears to be lots of color. When it fills up with people, they become the color factor. Thus the room looks attractive when it is empty and when it is full, and the color doesn't compete with the people. It is lit in such a way that the color dominates in the daytime and becomes more sedate at night. Artificial light is the key to controlling this dual effect. You can have color when you want it and dispense with it when you don't. Or for that matter, you can have a neutral shell and use colored lights, which is a more difficult solution.

Rooftop restaurants are understandably controversial. The food service is both expensive and difficult and so is the problem of getting people up and down without interfering with regular hotel traffic. In the Hancock Building in Chicago there is an elegant restaurant on the 95th floor, but it could be in the lobby. Much of the time it is in the clouds and you can't even see the city. I think rooftop facilities are great as cocktail lounges, but a rooftop restaurant for elegant dining doesn't seem worthwhile unless it is a "Windows on the World" atop New York's One World Trade Center where Warren Platner's design and the dramatic panorama prove an incomparable combination.

In terms of hotels, however, if it is to be done properly a complete kitchen is mandatory even with the simplest menu. Food is usually prepared in a central kitchen because of staffing problems. Why hire three people in three kitchens to do what one person can do in one kitchen? The food can be distributed from there. My point is that to attempt to make a rooftop restaurant into a Tour D'Argent invites failure. But if a simple lunch is served—a sandwich and glass of beer, for instance—hot hors d'oeuvres at cocktail time, and a simple one-plate dinner, a rooftop restaurant can be profitable. It seems to me, though, that a rooftop facility should really be more of a cocktail and nightclub type of place where food is ancillary to drinking.

Mr. Hargreaves of the Savoy Group in London has an interesting slant on rooftop restaurants (no pun intended). He says that "Many times over the last 60 or 70 years it has been debated whether the Savoy in London would be an ideal site for a roof restaurant with its views up and down the river. And each time, the board of the day has considered that it is not really viable. In this particular case, we haven't got the lifts . . . and would have to put them in for running the food up and refuse down, the people up and the staff down. This would mean abandoning a series of bedrooms . . . which all cut into the economics of the thing and consequently we have never done it. It was briefly debated whether we would have a rooftop restaurant at the new Berkeley overlooking Hyde Park but we decided instead to have a swimming pool up there and a small health club. So, we have debated it many times, but on the whole, we feel that it hasn't been worth it as far as we are concerned." While I agree with Mr. Hargreaves about rooftop restaurants, it is my opinion that a swimming pool would be just as costly, because of the structural difficulties, and less revenue producing.

Sir Charles Forte of the Trust Houses/Forte group says he is only in favor of rooftop restaurants "when it is a natural feature—when it has a wonderful view. Or if the hotel is so planned that the rooftop restaurant is part of the planning and an extension of the services of the hotel. I don't believe in rooftop restaurants simply because they are on the roof. If you sit in a rooftop restaurant, you are seldom aware of being in a rooftop restaurant. . . ."

Left: The nightclub in the Golden Sands Hotel in Fanagusta, Cypress

Below: The Pump Room in Chicago's Ambassador East Hotel.

Bottom: Cocktail lounge in the Hotel Marina Palace in Helsinki, Finland.

Right: The Cirque Restaurant Bar at the Mayfair House in New York takes its inspiration from French chateau interiors of the Louis XV period.

Below: Bar in the Bristol Place, a business and meeting hotel near the Toronto airport

COFFEE SHOPS

In a large hotel (700 to 1,000 rooms) or even a 400-room resort hotel, there might be three distinct restaurants—a "gourmet" dining room, a specialty restaurant, and a drug store or coffee shop. Each affords the guest a change of pace and a different menu. To most Americans the coffee shop implies a certain kind of food and fast service. It is an institution peculiar to the American hotel. It is a place where a businessperson can get a quick breakfast on the way to an appointment. Coffee shops traditionally have counters because theoretically seating and service are faster at a counter. In that respect today's coffee shop is not very different from the diner of the 1930s. Prices in the coffee shop are probably the lowest in the hotel, and most of them serve lunch and dinner as well as breakfast. The informality associated with the coffee shop makes it appealing to the man who doesn't want to put on a coat and the woman who prefers jeans. It is also a place where a family traveling with children can dine together.

As a general rule there should be more table space than counter space in a coffee shop. Counter space is wasteful. The backup that is needed steals footage from a room, but at the same time it is helpful to have a counter that can be kept open 24 hours a day. Planes arrive late and people often want something to eat when they arrive. While a hotel can't keep all its food facilities open all night, a skeleton staff can be kept in a coffee shop.

The designer's task is to keep the coffee shop from appearing sterile. Traditionally coffee shop floors were a hard surface—often terrazzo—so that the chairs could be stacked on the tables at night and the floors mopped. Now, however, there are manufactured fiber carpets that are soil resistant and easily maintainable. It is possible to have a highly styled carpet in the coffee shop with builtin acoustical and safety advantages.

Today's coffee shop not only provides all-day (and sometimes all-night) service, but can change its atmosphere to become a more leisurely place to dine. This can be achieved by lowering the light level, replacing table mats with table cloths, among other things. In a smaller hotel the coffee shop might be the only restaurant serving all purposes.

We are endeavoring to provide the coffee shop with a more elegant flavor not only through carpeting but also through wall covering and upholstery. A coffee shop, however, should not be too elegant or it loses its raison d'etre. Its design should be no-nonsense and without gimmicks. It should not try to emulate something totally remote from its function and appeal. Let it be what it is—an informal dining area with a feeling of cleanliness but not sterility. Bright colors and crisp forms suggest cleanliness. The treatment of the menu, dishes, and tableware can provide a strong identity.

CAFETERIAS

The cafeteria is a food service method that reduces personnel. The first hotel we were involved in for the Penta chain (part of an airline group which goes under the corporate name of European Hotel Corporation) is located opposite the British Airways Terminal in London. The main dining facility in the hotel is a cafeteria and the comparatively elegant atmosphere we achieved makes it atypical. Penta has a chain of moderate-priced hotels—"package" and businessmen's hotels—in Europe and they all incorporate cafeterias. The success of cafeterias, according to food and beverage consultant John Andrews, varies from country to country. In Sweden, for example, where breakfast is the smorgasbord, "it works quite nicely." But, he continues, "I don't like cafeterias. If I am eating in a restaurant I want to be served. But by the same token if it is speed one is interested in and the operation is efficient, cafeterias have their point." They are, however, more suited to airport and businesspeople's hotels than to a plush city or resort hotel, but that demarcation between the kind of hotel and type of clientele is becoming more vague.

Since the coffee shop, like other public areas of the airport hotel in Dublin, Ireland, is only one-story, it can be lighted from above. Ceilings here are rough timber diagonal sheeting with clusters of square roof lights.

Top: There is plenty of counter and table space in the busy coffee shop of the O'Hare Hilton at Chicago's O'Hare Airport.

Middle: The light and airy coffee shop at the Balmoral Beach Club in Nassau, West Indies, fits its island locale.

Bottom: The coffee shop in the Marina Palace Hotel in Helsinki, Finland, might be aboard ship.

LE DRUG STORE CONCEPT

The drug store concept might be called an idea, or at least a name, that has gone full circle. "Le Drug Store," pioneered in Paris with a name borrowed from the U.S., has now come back in French guise. The Paris Le Drug Store was designed by Slavik Designers and is a kind of merchandise happening. It combines food service, gift items, handbags and other accessories, record players, groceries, newspapers, and what have you, without any physical demarcation between one merchandising activity and another. The original Le Drug Store burned down and has been rebuilt on the Champs Elysées, and there are others throughout Europe.

We have experimented with a similar concept in several hotels, albeit in a more regimented form. A Le Drug Store might have food service kiosks with a different specialty in each—maybe Scandanavian food in one, Italian in another, American hot dogs and hamburgers in another, and so on. The decoration of each kiosk could suggest the country in which the food originated. In between the kiosks there might be a facility to vend greeting cards or all manner of merchandisable items. Since we have to make sure that the man who had a hot dog pays for it, it is necessary to establish physical boundaries for the food services. There are also health codes to comply with.

It is an exciting kind of space to design because it is not necessary to impose a so-called theme on the design. The theme is indigenous. It is something like an exhibition. It is difficult, however, to establish pathways so that a person who walks in the door can grasp the totality of the space, see where he wants to go, and has no difficulty getting there.

OUTDOOR AREAS

Usually one thinks of outdoor areas in relation to resort hotels, but to a certain extent the urban hotel should also include resort features. Resort amenities such as swimming pools, health clubs, and even indoor tennis courts could be included as a means of generating additional markets. Weekend guests from adjacent localities can also be attracted by such facilities.

How does or should the interior designer become involved with landscape, swimming pools, sports areas, health clubs—the complexities of a total environment? Where does the responsibility of the interior designer end? Designing a large hotel is a team effort. Each designer is a member of that team, each member respecting and understanding the input and capabilities of the others in order to complete the entire project. No designer can possess all the specialized skills which are required for the successful solution of a total design. He must have an awareness of his limitations.

OUTDOOR DINING

How does a designer deal with outdoor dining? First, by taking the climate and human psychology into consideration. At a ski resort, of course, it is too cold to dine out at night but it can be ideal in the middle of the day. In a hot climate where the hotels are air conditioned some women prefer not to dine outside at night because the humidity plays havoc with their hair. In that case the designer can create the illusion of an outdoor space by providing some invisible means of enclosure, such as a glass or plastic structure. By clever use of lighting, planting, and furnishings, there is seemingly no demarcation between outside and inside. Glass-enclosed dining areas were discussed in the section on rooftop facilities (see page 80).

Since climate limits outdoor dining even in the middle of the day, a temporary structure can be erected to keep inclement weather out, which can then be removed when not required. Dining outside, or even the illusion of being outside, is a pleasant experience especially in a natural environment complete with the sounds of the night.

Creativity is an instinctual process. As a designer, my best guage has always been my instincts. In the last analysis, a person's intuition is a much more potent barometer than any computer or statistician. As humans, we all have the ability to sense the human condition. Answers are within us, and it's a matter of trusting our own instincts. The most successful people in business acknowledge the necessity of playing hunches. The creative process of making designs stems from this same process: playing hunches. There are no guarantees, no formulas; only a kaleidoscope of possibilities from which to choose. Originality stems from the source within us and can happen only if we learn to draw on our own instincts.

Joan Saloomey

Tile-floored guest room in the Hyatt Rio Mar in Rio Grande/Luquille, Puerto Rico. The resort hotel consists of a cluster of balconied guest rooms, suites, and terraced villas.

GUEST ROOMS

Veteran foreign correspondent James Cameron, who has been a guest in many far-flung hotels, says he asks little of a bedroom "except that it have perfectly adjustable lighting, an impeccable telephone service, and total soundproofing. This is vital. Audible amatory exercises next door can be distracting if you are trying to read Hegel, say, and frustrating if you are not." Most hotel guests, however, are harder to please.

The guest room might be called the heart of the hotel. It is perhaps here more than anywhere else that the designer has to be aware of the comfort and well-being of the guest. Says Sheraton's Robert Kittner, "To the extent that the design team keeps the guest in mind as the number one person to serve, then they are on solid ground."

In the 19th century it was considered a luxury to have a gas lamp, a wash bowl, and a cake of soap in every room, but today's typical hotel guest expects a variety of amenities and luxuries that his 19th-century ancestor could hardly have imagined.

A guest, of course, is not so likely to notice comfort as he is the lack of it. We have to figure out how a guest will make use of his room and anticipate his needs. We try to place the light switch where he will expect it, the lighting for comfortable reading, the TV for easy viewing. The closet should have a parcel shelf, a val-pack hook, and functional, well-designed hangers. It is a matter of good manners. Good manners don't call attention to themselves, they simply exist.

The design of a guest room has to be approached differently than the design of public rooms. Scale in the lobby is larger-than-life; in the guest room it is life-size.

There are various types of guest rooms. The most requested are twin-bedded rooms and double rooms. Different hoteliers have their own ideas about the size of rooms and beds. The guest room in a resort hotel should be larger than the room in an urban hotel. Most rooms, however, should be double-bedded although there are various opinions about how large those beds should be—twins, queens, or kings. In a resort hotel the most popular might be a double-double room; that is, it has two beds each accommodating two people and is suited to a family on vacation. Or in another situation the ideal room might have a double and a king-size bed or two twin beds. A businessperson, however, might prefer a studio because it suggests the appearance of a living room which can be used for meetings. A variation on the studio is the bed that folds into the wall, thus providing additional space during the daytime.

European hoteliers tend to emphasize single rooms, but in my opinion a single room has builtin obsolescence. Although there may be a need for singles, Holiday Inns and other chains have demonstrated that the large bedroom with two full-size beds [4 ft 6 in (135 cm) each] is more economical. There is little you can do to make a small room larger. You can use optical devices such as mirrors to provide the appearance of size, but it can't be made to accommodate more than one guest.

Studio rooms were once highly popular with hoteliers because they don't look like bedrooms and are more attractive to walk into than a room consisting of wall-to-wall beds. But no matter how comfortable the bedding, no one has been able to overcome the psychological reluctance of sleeping on a sofa. There may be a need for some studios, but I think they should be kept to a minimum. They are more satisfactory as a connecting room that makes up a suite.

Robert Kittner of Sheraton is of the opinion (although it isn't entirely in agreement with Sheraton's) that the studio room is anathema. "I wouldn't put any studio rooms in a hotel. It isn't a good sofa and it isn't a good bed. I think the ideal solution would be to have oversize guest rooms —maybe 14 feet wide by 24 feet long—with a definite lounge area. The percentage of these rooms would depend on the hotel but in a commercial

Left: A bedroom in Habitation Leclerc, an exotic resort in Port-au-Prince, Haiti, which was once the estate of Napoleon's sister, Pauline Bonaparte Leclerc.

Below: Another bedroom in Habitation Leclerc.

Top: One of three bedroom design concepts—
American Empire, Eastlake, and Faux Bamboo—
at the Rye Town Hilton in Rye, New York. They
were designed to create the impression of bedrooms in a country house.

Middle: An example of the uncompromisingly
modern bedrooms at the Marquette Inn in Minneapolis's IDS Center. Larger than standard hotel
rooms, they're about the size of a typical motel
bedroom.

Bottom: Bedroom in Club Mediterranee in
Cancun, Mexico.

Opposite page: A typical brick-vaulted bedroom
at the Hammamet Sheraton in Tunisia. All rooms
in this Mediterranean hotel of 1- and 2-story
buildings are staggered, each facing the sea.

hotel I would think there should be as many as 20 percent of this type of room."

Gulf Hotels, according to Norman Anderson, are designing guest rooms with either one 50-in. (127 cm) bed or two queen-size beds. Some of the latter also have a studio bed which acts as a settee in a sitting area separated by a divider.

Hyatt International has developed a system that eliminates communicating doors on the party wall between guest rooms. A vestibule incorporating two sets of doors makes it possible to use the two rooms separately or as a connecting suite. When the outer set of doors is locked, the two rooms comprise a suite connecting through the vestibule. When the room is individually rented, the vestibule becomes part of the public corridor. This system has proven highly successful. For the person who rents a single room, it is comforting not to have a communicating door within the room. For the designer it is advantageous to have an uncluttered wall elevation for furniture.

There is a tendency for guest rooms to become smaller because of rising costs. Suppose a hotel room costs around $40 a square foot to build and 1 ft or 30 cm is cut from its length, the saving would be about 10 or 12 sq ft per room. In a 1,000-room hotel the saving would be 12,000 sq ft times $40—nearly half a million dollars.

Ordinarily the width of a room is fairly constant—12 to 14 ft (3.6 to 4.3 m)—and the depth is from 16 to 18 ft (4.8 to 5.5 m). An average bedroom (exclusive of bathroom, closet, and dressing room) is usually 12 by 16 ft (3.6 by 4.8 m) or 12 by 17 ft (3.6 by 5.1 m), which relates to construction economics. There are, however, ways of cutting down on footage while retaining the illusion of space. For example, the window end of the room might be wedge shaped, prow shaped, or a kind of bay where two triangles have been sliced off each side. Not only does this overcome the "shoebox" effect but the cost saving factor is considerable. We usually place a table and two chairs within that triangular space. This makes an attractive focal point in the room and the table can be used for room service, as a desk, or as a dressing table near daylight.

We are also experimenting with the scale of furniture. The proper use of color and materials can make fairly large pieces of furniture appear smaller. Many hotel operators are using a queen-size bed, which is 60 in. (152.4 cm) wide, and renting the room as a king-size room. A king-size bed is 78 in. (198.1 cm).

Another way of saving space is by using vertical instead of horizontal furniture. The case goods in a guest room are usually strung along the wall opposite the beds. Now we have pieces that are reminiscent of an updated armoire, but instead of being a closet, they have a bureau and a retractable desk facility in the lower part. In the upper part is a TV that swivels and is high enough to be viewed comfortably from the bed. Above the TV is a storage compartment for extra pillows and blankets. And at the very top there might be a light that illuminates the room indirectly. But while this multipurpose piece of furniture saves space, it can appear sterile. We have tried to compensate for this through the selection of richer materials, carpets, and art work. Modern fabric technology has made it possible to use light colors that can withstand many launderings and cleanings without fading.

In any case I think there is usually too much furniture in hotel guest rooms. Chests contain too many drawers which are rarely used. Today's average guest travels by air and therefore travels light. If he takes a garment bag it is hung in the closet and other clothes are put on coat hangers. The closet in today's room need only be large enough to provide suitable hanging space with possibly some drawer space and a place to store luggage. A large walk-in closet is only appropriate when it becomes part of a dressing area.

Beds are standard sizes in most countries. Linens, bedspreads, and

In this bedroom at the Nassau Beach Hotel in Nassau, West Indies, the usual hotel case pieces strung against the wall have been replaced by a vertical armoirelike piece containing drawers and television.

headboards are all geared to those sizes. I don't know how they evolved—whether from the length of the king from the top of his head to his toes or whether from manufacturing companies. The twin bed probably derived from European measurements. The American twin bed is 39 in. (99.1 cm) wide, which approximately equals 1 m. Beds were traditionally 75 in. (190.5 cm) long until people started growing taller and now they are 78 in. (198.1 cm) or 6½ ft (2 m). The so-called American "king-size bed" is actually a 6½ ft square. The queen-size bed is 60 in. (152.4 cm) wide. The classic double bed is 4½ ft (1.4 m) wide. In addition to the 39 in. (99.1 cm) twin bed there is also a 3 ft (91.4 cm) bed which probably derived from school dormitory beds. These dimensions are universal. The so-called "Bahama" bed used in studio rooms is actually a twin bed placed lengthwise against the wall with deep bolsters or pillow storage space to provide back supports.

Lighting in guest rooms is important for a number of reasons. It is important in helping to create the environment the designer intended and in giving the guest a sense of well-being. This is particularly important in a city hotel where the guest room draperies are usually drawn and to all intents and purposes it is an interior space. Lighting, of course, must also provide comfortable illumination for reading, working, and applying cosmetics.

We have experimented with a variety of lighting solutions in guest rooms. In some cases we have downlight over a table and chair arrangement. In the same room we will also have indirect light—that might be built into the furniture—to provide an overall glow. We have developed bed lights that have special baffles so they can be used by one person without creating glare for another person in the bed. We are also developing switching schemes so that when the room door is unlocked a light turns on, and it can also be switched off from the bed. A guest room, like many areas in a hotel, should have good illumination but it should not be overlit. "We are an overlit society," says Howard Brandston, "that uses far more light than is necessary for eye comfort or efficient task performance."

Traditional bedroom in the Royal Sonesta in New Orleans, Louisiana.

The geometry of the room dictates how many light sources there should be and whether or not the source of light is a sculptural object that serves as decor, or the source is unseen by the guest and the room just seems to glow with its own light, or whether it is a combination of these. There might be light within a piece of furniture that is directed toward the ceiling and thus creates enough reflected illumination in the room for a guest to find his way around and watch television. There might be light inside a closet with a louvered door that emits enough illumination to serve as a night light.

We are developing systems in which light and furniture are integrated—the lamp and the table, for instance. There is a night table that is integrated with the bed. It has a back plate that matches the headboard with a lamp mounted on the back plate. This makes it possible to keep the top surface of the night table free for ashtray, phone, clock radio, television controls, and so on—all designed and integrated into the unit.

Some hotel operators request five or six color schemes for guest rooms so they can offer guests a choice. If, however, a guest asks for a blue room and none is available, he is disappointed. But if the guest rooms are all one color scheme, the guest has no choice. I see no reason why there should be more than one color scheme for all typical guest rooms in a hotel and never more than two. If a color scheme works well for one room, it should work well for all rooms. One color scheme, moreover, simplifies maintenance and housekeeping. There is no danger that a blue bedspread will wind up in a green room or a red chair in a blue room. It also saves on the initial investment since buying greater numbers of each item makes for economical purchasing. We are designing hotels with as many as a thousand rooms with one color scheme. But of course suites can and should have a very special character.

There are, of course, sometimes valid reasons for a hotel to feature individuality in its guest rooms. When the new Berkeley was built in London, several interior designers were employed for the guest rooms with the avowed object of having a variety of schemes. "The feeling we wished to convey at that particular hotel," as Mr. Hargreaves puts it, "was that every single room was differently designed."

Designers often hesitate to use bold color in guest rooms because they are afraid of the public response. But a hotel bedroom is unlike a residential bedroom. A hotel is a transitory experience. If it is executed with taste, a guest won't find bold color and pattern overpowering as he might in his own bedroom. It is the designer's responsibility to make the world a more attractive place to be whether he starts with a hotel bedroom, the menu, the uniforms, or the entrance door. We should make every endeavor to improve the attractiveness of everything we touch. People often respond to something that is attractive or has been defined attractive by designers. I don't think people are born with bad taste and have to be educated out of it. They are born with no taste and can be educated to good taste.

Designers of today's guest rooms might do well to heed the words of *New York Times* architectural critic Ada Louise Huxtable who says she never approaches a trip requiring an overnight stay without a sinking heart. "It's not that I won't be reasonably comfortable . . . basic things like beds and ice and Coke machines are the preoccupation of the American hospitality industry. It's that I will be so depressed. It is not the impersonality or anonymity of a hotel room . . . it is that one is forced into a banal, standardized, multi-billion-dollar world of bad colors, bad fabrics, bad prints, bad pictures, bad furniture, bad lamps, bad ice buckets, and bad wastebaskets of such totally uniform and cheap consistency of taste and manufacture that borax would be an exhilarating change of pace."

I believe in designing a hotel guest room and making a prototype of the guest room and bathroom before furnishings are purchased. Then all

. . . A hotel pays a great deal of attention to its bathroom appurtenances—a direct ratio existing between the size of the bill and what is made available in the bathroom.

George Plimpton

Top: Bath in one of the villas at Habitation Leclerc in Port-au-Prince, Haiti.

Bottom: Bathroom at the Tower House in Miami Beach, Florida.

mistakes and adjustments can be corrected. A single mistake in the guest room of a 1,000-room hotel is multiplied a thousand times!

Balconies are a feature of many hotels. While they may be attractive from the outside they are rarely used. Since air conditioning makes it necessary to keep windows closed, it isn't to the hotel's advantage to have a balcony. It does, however, tend to make the guest room seem larger and in a resort hotel a balcony might be used for breakfast. Balconies are useless in urban hotels. No one is going to go out on a wind-blown terrace 30 stories above a noisy city street.

BATHROOMS

"Of all the many ways in which American domestic life has been influenced by hotels, the influence of the hotel bathroom stands pre-eminent," says Jefferson Williamson in *The American Hotel, An Anecdotal History* of 1930. "Every room with bath," he adds, "has been a proud boast of a great many American hotels since the 1890s." And yet the bathroom is a neglected area of today's hotel. It is also the place that can make the greatest impression on a guest. No matter how elegant the guest room, a guest will discredit a hotel if the bathroom is outmoded or the fixtures are worn or damaged.

Physically the bathroom is becoming smaller because of building costs. The bathroom, therefore, should be planned with the greatest care. It is, in fact, the most complicated and time-consuming area to design. A bathroom is a tiny cubicle of space, but it involves such an army of trades, including rough plasterers, finished plasterers, tile setters, plumbers, electricians, carpenters, shop finishers, marble setters, painters . . . that it could be done a lot better in the factory. There is no technological reason why bathrooms cannot be prefabricated and dropped into place.

SUITES

Suites have been a feature of hotels ever since the Tremont opened in Boston in 1829 to astound the world with its luxuries, including ten parlors each with a connecting bed chamber. Today's suites are designed just as they were then for the guest who wants more palatial accommodations and also for the executive who uses it as a place for meetings and small parties during a convention. There is a tendency to put suites on one floor —preferably the top floor or penthouse floor, as it is often named—and devote the entire space to them. In that way the guest feels as if he is receiving VIP treatment by being segregated. When all the suites are on one floor it is also possible to provide extra services that the average guest would not have. If suites are not segregated by floor they should be located at the corners of the hotel where there is more fenestration, where they are away from the elevators, and where they can be connected to typical rooms as necessary.

Deluxe suite in the Host Hotel in Houston, Texas.

Left: Suite in the Chosun Hotel in Seoul, Korea.

Below: Suite in the Kiawah Inn in Atlanta, Georgia.

Right: Bedroom area in a typical suite in the Sheraton Buenos Aires in Venezuela.

Below: Suite in the renovated Whitehall Hotel in Chicago.

Opposite page top: An electronic system called Cardgard, which is installed at New York's Algonquin Hotel, provides for guest room security without the use of conventional locks and keys. When a guest checks out, his card code is canceled.

Opposite page bottom: Setbacks on the exterior of the Marquette Inn in Minneapolis's IDS Center are reflected in the interior. The rooms on each floor are stepped back to give most a corner view, and the zig-zag is reiterated on the inner wall of the rooms and in the corridor, turning what is often a long, boring space into an exciting one.

GUEST ROOM CORRIDORS

Corridors are long passageways with guest rooms usually on both sides. The designer's aim is to reduce their visual length and make the corridor as attractive as possible so that today's hotel guest won't react as Mrs. Trollope did when she visited the Eagle Hotel in Buffalo in the 1830s and described it as having "all the pretension of a splendid establishment, but its monstrous corridors, low ceilings, and intricate chambers, gave me the feeling of a catacomb...."

There are several ways to break up the long, narrow spaces with changes of carpet design, changes of lighting, and changes of ceiling height. The guest room doors might also be recessed. A corridor is devoid of furniture except for the elevator foyer where the treatment should be distinctive.

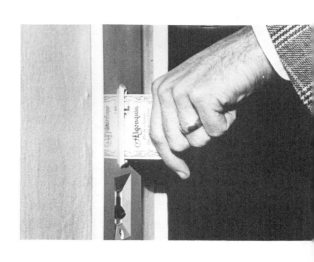

6. Hotel Rehabilitation

"The most serious mistake that hotel/motel owners can make is to stop updating and remodeling, which is a fact of life in the business," is the way Charles Hall, Vice President and Director of Design of the Revere Group, Washington, D.C., expressed it in the April 1975 *Contract* magazine. "To wait until money is less costly may result in revenue losses due to competition."

Updating and remodeling has always been a fact of life in the hotel business. The Tremont, America's first modern hotel, was modernized twice during its 65 years. In 1852 its plumbing facilities were extended to every part of the hotel, among other improvements, and in 1889 it was equipped with electric lights and other up-to-date features. The importance of remodeling was even noted by Sinclair Lewis in *Work of Art,* his fictionalized account of the American hotel business in which an "honest country inn" in Connecticut found it necessary toward the end of the 19th century to keep abreast of the times by putting in bathrooms, turning the stable into a garage, and generally refurbishing. A "brisk little lady from a Hartford department store" looked "with dislike upon the spittoons and honest old scruffy leather chairs in the lobby, the equally honest iron beds and straight chairs in the bedroom. . . ." And "in place of the straight, respectable lines of chairs along the walls" of the lobby, "she put in a nasty mixture of wicker chairs with cretonne cushions, and leather chairs that weren't rockers. . . . She reduced the lordly desk to a mere nook in a corner, and hid the key rack. And in the bedroom she installed still other despicable wicker chairs, and painted pine bedsteads without one ornamental iron curlicue. But it was the dining room that she most disfigured," in the eyes of the manager. "She got rid of the long, solid, satisfactory tables and put in small separate tables—with red tops —on which, she directed, not luxurious thick cotton tablecloths but dinky little doilies were to be used; and the wall she painted a shrieking yellow."

But whether it is Sinclair Lewis's fictionalized turn-of-the-century country inn or a big contemporary metropolitan hotel, rehabilitation is essential if it is to retain its prestige. New merchandising areas have to be incorporated within the structure. Technological innovations have to be installed. Fashions in such things as fabrics, furniture, and decor also change, of course, but it is rash to be too fashionable in that sense. It takes as long as four years to build some hotels and what was fashionable when construction started might be a cliche when it is completed. I believe that a well-designed hotel interior should last 10 years or more. Interior designer Norman De Haan, AIA, points out in the July 1975 *AIA Journal* that when the exterior of a building is completed, it is generally fixed almost forever, but its interior is something that people not only work and live *in,* but work *on.* To effectively plan interior spaces, he adds, changed patterns of use must be anticipated.

Too many hotel owners refurbish where it shows rather than where it is needed, which is usually the lobby. The hotel lobby, as Charles Hall of Revere puts it, "is a hotel's best selling point and it has to be a show stopper. If customer's don't like what they see at that point they will never make it to the registration desk."

Opposite page: Amsterdam's Amstel Hotel boasts one of the most splendid entrance halls and staircases in any hotel in Europe. Completed in 1866 and recently renovated, this grand old hotel has been graced by kings and queens, princes and princesses, presidents and prime ministers.

Above: The ceiling of the Amstel's grand entrance hall.

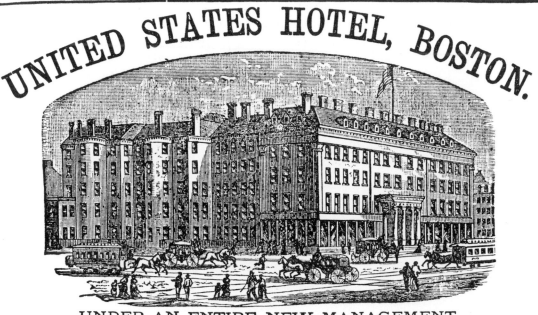

UNITED STATES HOTEL, BOSTON.

UNDER AN ENTIRE NEW MANAGEMENT.

REPAINTED, REFURNISHED, & GREATLY IMPROVED

By an expenditure during the past six months of over ☞ **$50,000!**

New Passenger Elevator, Electric Bells, a perfect system of Sewerage and Ventilation, and every convenience that health and comfort can suggest. Located

DIRECTLY OPPOSITE THE BOSTON AND ALBANY,

AND ONLY ONE BLOCK FROM THE

OLD COLONY AND FALL RIVER LINES, three blocks only from the NEW YORK AND NEW ENGLAND, and PROVIDENCE AND STONINGTON STATIONS, and connecting directly by HORSE CARS, EVERY 5 MINUTES, with all the Northern and Eastern Railroads and Steamboats, giving Guests every possible facility and convenience of rapid and economical transfer from all points.

☞ UNEQUALLED BY ANY HOTEL IN BOSTON.

Passengers to or from all *Southern* or *Western Points*, by either *Boat* or *Rail*, MAY SAVE ALL CARRIAGE FARES.

ITS CENTRAL LOCATION,

BEING IN THE BUSY TRADE CENTRE OF ALL THE

Great Mercantile Establishments, Elegant Shopping, Theatres,
Post-Office, Custom House, and all Places of Amusement,

AND EVERY OBJECT OF INTEREST,

MAKES IT ALTOGETHER THE MOST ACCESSIBLE AND CONVENIENT HOTEL IN THE CITY.

EVERYTHING NEW FRESH, CLEAN, and COMFORTABLE.

The notable character of its Guests, its Unexceptionable Table, its Broad Halls, and Grand Old Parlors, all recommend the UNITED STATES as possessing more substantial comforts than any Hotel in Boston, and offers to Guests, either permanent or transient, the

Largest Variety of Spacious Rooms, and the most Liberal Scale of Prices.

PLEASURE PARTIES, LADIES AND FAMILIES

visiting or passing through the City, may secure Rooms with or without Meals, and will find every attention at the UNITED STATES, the nearest first-class Hotel to all the Great Retail Stores; having Waiting and Toilet Rooms, Ladies' Package Room, and every convenience.

☞ Comfort, Courtesy, and Moderate Charges are the Virtues of Hotel Life.

The UNITED STATES fills these requirements in a most marked and successful degree.

Regular Transient Rates, for full Day's Board, Single Rooms,	$2.50
Rooms alone,	1.00
Single Meals,	.75
Parlors, Outside or Double Rooms and Baths,	$3 to $4 per day

Rooms may be engaged with or without Meals.

Special Rates will be made for Large Parties or Permanent Guests.

☞ *Orders for Rooms by Mail or Telegraph promptly attended to.*

TILLY HAYNES, Proprietor.

ISAAC N. ANDREWS, Manager.

Most hotel and motel remodeling is done by cycle, so that some part of the hotel is almost continually being renovated. Guest rooms, in general, should be remodeled about every 5 years. Carpet should be replaced more often than anything else in a guest room. If the carpet is worn or stained, everything in the room appears dingy. Therefore, I believe, as do many hotel owners and operating companies, that one should use inexpensive carpet in guest rooms so it can be replaced often. Hard surface materials might seem to be a more practical flooring for guest rooms, but there is a builtin expectancy among hotel guests, particularly Americans, of stepping on carpet when they get out of bed. And carpet, in any case, is more economical than tile flooring. The guest room floor in a resort hotel, however, might be ceramic or vinyl tile because of the sense of coolness it imparts.

The rising cost of new building is certain to result in even more rehabilitation in the coming years. That some of the grand old hotels have shown a remarkable ability not only to survive but also to thrive has made their renovation both feasible and fashionable. What preservationists have not been able to do, rising building costs may accomplish. The value of rehabilitation, however, depends on several factors. It depends on the reputation of the hotel. If that has suffered, renovation will be of little use. Or if it is in a location, for instance, where traffic and parking are a problem, rehabilitation will be useless. But rehabilitation can only enhance the reputation of an elegant old hotel that has never lost its prestige. The Plaza in New York, the Savoy in London, the St. Francis in San Francisco are but a few examples that come immediately to mind.

Renovating a fine old hotel can be a rewarding experience. Designer Dale Keller told *Contract* magazine in its November 1975 issue that a lot of his work is renovating, particularly "old classic hotels." While admitting that the cost is high, the indirect advantage is "the romance of it, the nostalgic benefit that is so easy to promote." Although, he added, room rates may be higher, "the old hotel is always the prestige place to stay." Keller told about modernizing the Taj Mahal in Bombay, which was done in the thirties "in a kind of bad Art Deco." Behind it was "a kind of Gothic-Victorian-Indian style," which, says Keller, "was superb. We restored it; stripped all the paint off the woodwork in the corridors to get back to the wood, solid teak. The restoration was very exciting for everybody."

If it is an old hotel with character, that character must be preserved for that is where its economic advantage lies. Apply appropriate decor by all means without necessarily refacing everything, but do not modernize. The emphasis should always be on merchandising the hotel's image. That is probably what foreign correspondent James Cameron meant when he said he classified hotels "much as I am told wine lovers define claret, less for their appearance than for their bouquet."

Another kind of rehabilitation is recycling old buildings, originally designed for other purposes, into hotels. Just as self-made hotelier José Tjurs recycled old bordellos in Rio into new hotels, several big international hotel chains are converting a variety of old buildings into modern hotels. Holiday Inns have recycled a group of old houses in Bruges, Belgium, into a hotel. The Sonestis Hotel in Amsterdam uses a 17th-century church as its conference center. Hilton International is incorporating an ancient monastery and church tower in Budapest into a new hotel, which is to have a modern addition faced with mirror glass to reflect its historic locale. The Henry Villard houses in midtown New York, designed in the 1880s by McKim, Mead, & White in an Italian Renaissance style, are to be incorporated into a new hotel tower.

How is it possible for a great, or even a good, hotel to be created by a committee? All committees can do is to check out what has been proved successful in the past and repeat it. For over two decades, a wedge has been driven between the professional designer who is designing or renovating a hotel, and the hotel administrator, who has to operate the hotel.

James Nassikas, Stanford Court Hotel, San Francisco

Woodcut of a poster advertisement for the United States Hotel in Boston in the late 19th century. Courtesy Bettmann Archive.

Rendering of the Palace Hotel, a renovation of the Henry Villard houses in midtown New York, designed in the 1880s by McKim, Mead, & White in an Italian Renaissance style.

HOTEL ST. FRANCIS IN SAN FRANCISCO, CALIFORNIA

San Francisco's 1907 Hotel St. Francis retains its Edwardian elegance while a thoroughly modern 32-story annex looming behind it looks from Union Square as if it were a separate building.

Above: Living-dining room of the Shangri-La
Suite. The 31st floor of the Hotel St. Francis annex is entirely devoted to six suites, each individually decorated.

Right: Bayview Suite entrance.

Left: A suite bathroom.
Below: Living-dining room of the Bayview Suite.

ST. LOUIS HOTEL IN NEW ORLEANS, LOUISIANA

The original St. Louis Hotel in New Orleans where plantation owners came for the season was burned early in this century. Its memory and elegance, however, have been revived in a new St. Louis in the Vieux Carre. All its 75 rooms face an interior courtyard of the type that inspired John Portman. Reproductions of Louis XV and XVI, Directoire, and Empire periods have been used throughout the public rooms.

Left: The courtyard at night.
Below: The lobby.

WHITEHALL HOTEL IN CHICAGO

The original Whitehall in Chicago was a run-down residential hotel, but it boasted one of the city's best private club restaurants, which kept the hotel alive. When it was decided to rehabilitate it as an intimate urban hotel, the interior was gutted and many of the original 2-room suites were made into singles. This necessitated new fenestration, new bathrooms, and new lighting.

Above: A renovated suite.

Right: Typical guest room.

Opposite page: Another type of suite.

Left: European royalty, international celebrities, and the famed coquettes of the 1890s walked under this chandelier, which hangs from a domed ceiling in the entrance hall of the Hotel de Paris in Monte Carlo, Monaco. The hotel opened in 1864, less than a year after the Monte Carlo Casino with which it has always been associated.

Opposite page: The tower of the Hotel St. Francis in San Francisco.

Right: The lobby of the Inter-Continental Hotel in Maui, Hawaii, for which designers Howard Hirsch & Associates created a sophisticated Polynesian atmosphere compatible with the tropical environment. The intention, says designer Hirsch, "was to impart to visitors the impression that they were specially invited guests at a magnificent Hawaiian villa."

Below: The Hyatt Regency Brussels in Belgium is a fine example of a hotel that was built from the inside out. The registration desk and lobby are shown here.

Eighteenth-century Adam elegance is evoked in
the lounge and public areas of the otherwise
modern Howard Hotel in London.

Above: A high ceiling and wide views of the Gulf of Mexico are features of the main floor lobby of the Marco Beach Hotel on Marco Island, off Florida's west coast.

Right: Cylindrical elevators carry guests through the atrium of the Hyatt Regency Caspian in Chalus, Iran, to their room level. Behind the camera is the pool and patio area and views of the Caspian Sea.

Opposite page top: The vast lobby of the Heathrow Hotel at London's Heathrow Airport was designed to appeal to the international business and holiday travelers the hotel caters to.

Opposite page bottom: Staircase and corridor in the Heathrow Hotel at London's airport.

Opposite page: Staircase rising from the lobby of the Host Hotel in Houston.

Left: The Hyatt Regency Brussels ballroom is a multipurpose space which can be divided into small meeting rooms.

Below: The terrace dining room at the Xanadu Yacht & Tennis Club in the Grand Bahamas features a Tiffany-like Plexiglas in the center of the floor which is lit from below. The room is transformed into a discotheque in the evening.

Above: The George Bar at the Holiday Inn Marble Arch in London.

Opposite page top: The bar and cocktail lounge in the Hyatt Regency Brussels.

Opposite page bottom: The bar and cocktail area adjoin the gambling casino at the Hyatt Regency Caspian in Chalus, Iran.

Above: The coffee shop at the Hyatt Regency Brussels follows the "Le Drug Store Concept" and is interrelated with various types of small shops and boutiques. The food served represents various countries and regions—the American "Fountain," the Pizza Bar, the Scandinavian "Open" Sandwich, and a section devoted to Franco-Belgian pastries to take out. This is an entrance into the coffee shop from the street which does not interfere with hotel traffic.

Right: A detail of the coffee shop counter in the Hyatt Regency Brussels.

Opposite page: The living room of one of the smaller duplex suites at the U.N. Plaza Hotel in New York. The spiral staircase leads to the bedroom.

Above: The living room of a suite at the Hyatt Regency Brussels.

Right: The living room of a suite in the Tower House in Miami, Florida.

Opposite top: This mock-up shows a typical guest room designed for the Sheraton Karachi in Pakistan while it was under construction. Not only does a mock-up of a guest room make it possible for owners and management to see the designer's concept as no drawing or perspective could, but it allows the designer to check any problems, such as the placement of lighting and height of furniture, long before purchases are made.

Opposite page bottom: Typical guest room at the Sheraton Dubai on the Arabian Gulf.

This indoor pool has an outdoor ambiance at the
Holiday Inn Swiss Cottage in London.

This indoor pool is at the Holiday Inn Marble
Arch in London.

The dramatic sweep of the entrance of the Hyatt Regency Caspian in Chalus, Iran, greets the hotel's visitors.

THE RITZ IN LONDON

The London Ritz has occupied its present Picadilly/Green Park site since it opened in 1906 with such grand hotel amenities as Louis XVI fountains and lovely ceiling paintings in its public rooms, marble mantelpieces in the bedrooms, and bathrooms the size of most of today's bedrooms. A recent restoration by its new owners, Trafalgar House, a large conglomerate which also owns Cunard, Cementation Construction Company, among other major properties, is intended to turn a landmark into a tourist-oriented hotel.

Above: Suite living room.

Left: Private dining room.

STANFORD COURT IN SAN FRANCISCO

Stanford Court on San Francisco's Nob Hill is a new hotel with a grand hotel ambience. It was created within the original shell of the Stanford Court Apartments built in 1912 on the site of the Leland Stanford Mansion, which was destroyed by the 1906 earthquake. The 1912 brick-paved porte-cochère was retained, and a stained glass dome and fountain have been added to this grand entrance.

Above: Exterior.

Right: Stained glass dome above the fountain in the brick-paved porte-cochère.

Opposite page: A 19th-century Baccarat crystal chandelier hangs above a pair of settees in the foyer.

PLAZA HOTEL IN NEW YORK

New York's Plaza Hotel is one of the storied hotels on this side of the Atlantic. The French Renaissance building was designed by Henry Hardenbergh, who is responsible for several of America's great turn-of-the-century hotels, including the spectacular 1892 Waldorf Hotel in New York and the Copley-Plaza in Boston. Ever since the Plaza opened in 1907, it has harbored a colorful international clientele since it was taken over by Western International Hotels in 1974, it has undergone a $10 million refurbishing program.

Below: The Plaza insignia in a doorway.

Right: The famous Palm Court.

Bottom: The Edwardian Room.

Opposite page: A corridor adjacent to the Palm Court.

7. Design Procedures and Techniques

The object of a presentation, of course, is to display a product whether it is the interior design of a 1,000-room hotel, a magazine article, or a lighting system as clearly and as attractively as possible. In the case of the hotel the way the designer presents his ideas to the client is of paramount importance. The form of his presentation, the degree to which it visually communicates what the designer intends to convey, its graphic appeal can all spell the difference between success and failure.

After the feasibility study has been accomplished and the financing has been set for a new hotel, the owner or the operator (rarely are the owner and operator the same person) has an outline prepared of the scope of work involved. This includes the type of clientele the client wants to appeal to, the number and kind of bedrooms and what they will rent for, the public spaces and amenities required—in short, the individual areas for which an interior designer's services will be required.

We then make a contract proposal based on the client's requirements, which explains the particular services to be rendered. This may include any standard design services or a combination of services such as interior design, lighting design, landscaping, and product purchasing.

After the client accepts the contract proposal, preliminary schematic plans are presented. These may include layouts, furniture and/or equipment locations, finishes, and other specifics related directly to the function of the project.

Then the final design concept presentation is made to the client. This covers every aspect of the project through renderings, photographs, material samples and presentation boards. Budgets are also reviewed.

Although a designer may not be particularly articulate with words, he can be articulate with his design which ought to speak for itself. Even if a designer can sell a job by talking, it should all be spelled out in the presentation.

When making a presentation it is valuable to know something about the people you are selling to. If, however, you are dealing with a large chain, you may find yourself making the presentation to as many as 15 or 20 people—from food service, management, back-of-the-house, public relations, and so on—and psychology is little help. Your presentation has to be understood by all if it is to sell the job for you. It can be a mistake to show blueprints because fewer people than would care to admit it can read a blueprint. Therefore some technique should be used so that even laypeople can readily visualize a room or area. Audiovisual techniques might include showing slides on two screens—one for floor plans, the other for renderings of the space.

After the preliminaries are agreed to, it is the designer's responsibility to carry through the program—to provide interiors that work functionally as well as esthetically within an agreed budget. First, he analyzes the building and decides traffic patterns—how guests will enter, where they will go, how the various spaces will be used. A hotel is a series of spaces that must be considered as a unit and at the same time each area must be designed for its particular use and have its own atmosphere and yet become an integral part of the whole.

You have to believe in it, accepting the fact that it's very difficult, that there is a greater mass of detailed work to be mastered and handled than in other aspects of architectural work. It is considerably more difficult to maintain control over an interior project than, for example, over construction work. Every client thinks he knows something about it, and makes his own judgment. As a consequence, it becomes difficult to maintain a consistent style.

Warren Platner, FAIA

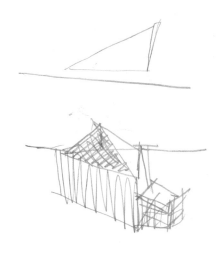

Model of the Hyatt Regency Karachi, a tourist/business/convention hotel under construction in Karachi.

Above: Model of the Sheraton Dubai on the
Arabian Gulf.

Opposite page: Model of the Hyatt Regency
Caspian, a resort in Chalus, Iran.

He must decide what areas to emphasize and what areas to subdue. Lighting can help create the various moods of the different areas and the change of pace from one to another so that as the guest walks through the hotel there is excitement as well as unity. The lighting designer, according to Howard Brandston, "reinforces what the interior designer has done."

It is the designer's art to make guests feel they are in a glamorous place and the lighting designer's art to orchestrate that glamor. Hotels are "hardly 'total works of art' in the Wagnerian sense," admits hotel architect Herbert Weisskamp, "for though their architecture, like Wagner's scores, may bear up the whole, it will also be dominated by action, by decor and by stage-management."

A hotel should be designed to be understood quickly. A guest who stays for two days or one who spends two hours in a restaurant or cocktail lounge should have an impression of something pleasurable.

It is also the designer's function to merchandise the various areas of the hotel whether it be restaurants, cocktail lounges, bars, or supper clubs. A hotel, as Brandston puts it, "is a very special place not just a building." And that is what the guest should feel.

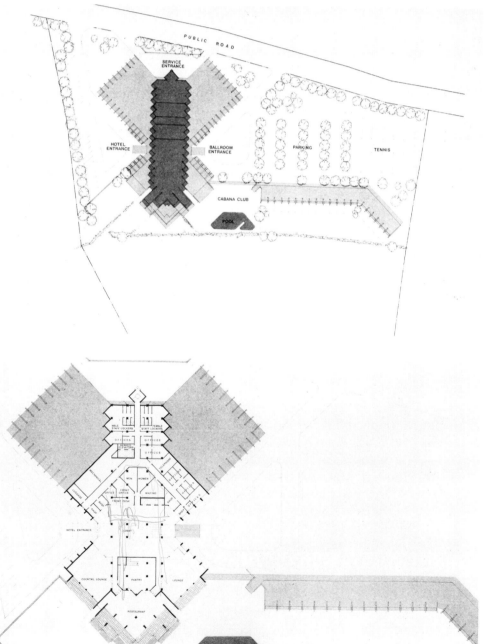

HYATT OCHO RIOS HOTEL IN OCHO RIOS, JAMAICA, WEST INDIES

Top: Model of a resort area currently being overdeveloped.

Middle: Site plan.

Bottom: Lobby floor plan.

Opposite page top: Typical guest floor plan.

Opposite page middle: Typical guest rooms.

Opposite page bottom: End suites.

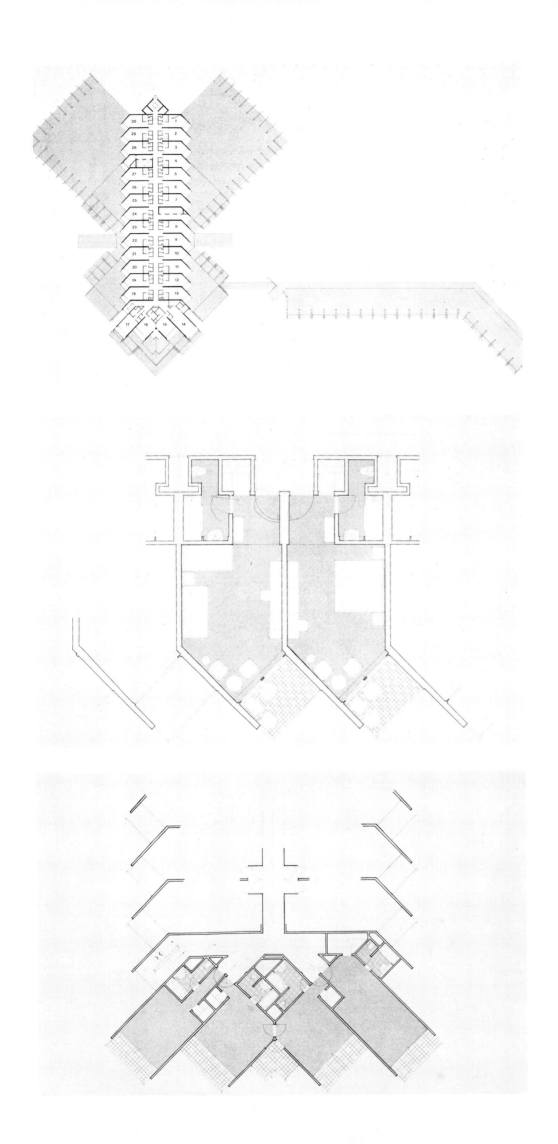

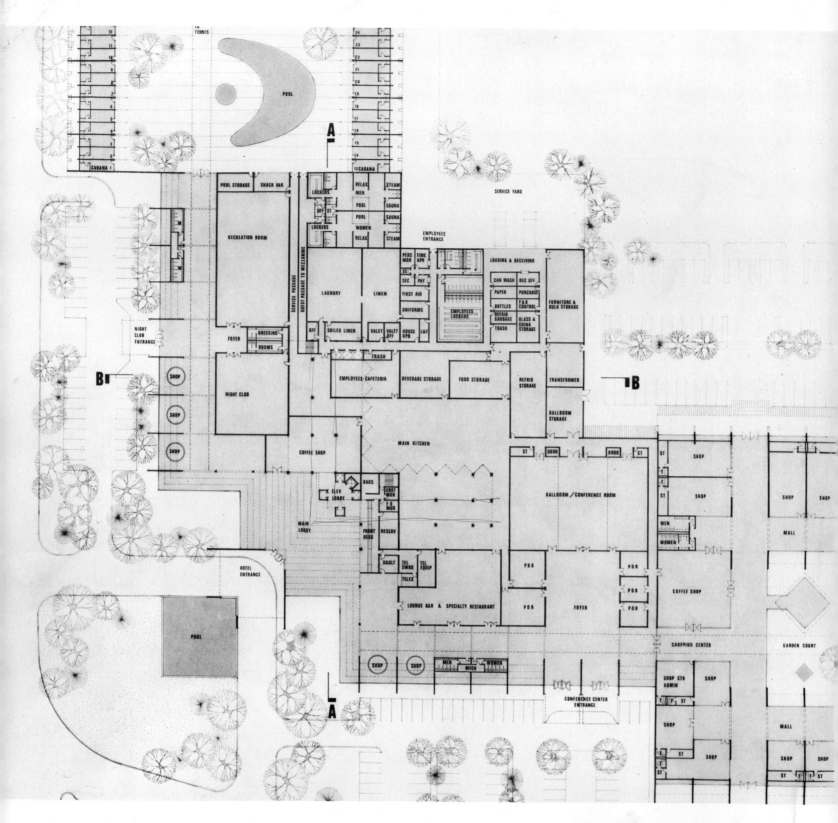

BAHRAIN SHERATON IN MIDDLE EAST
Above: Ground floor plan of the business/tourist hotel.

Opposite page top: Typical layout of a guest room floor.

Opposite page bottom: Typical guest rooms.

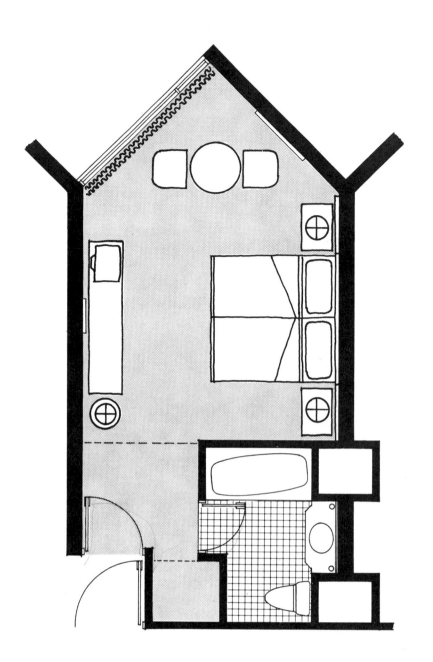

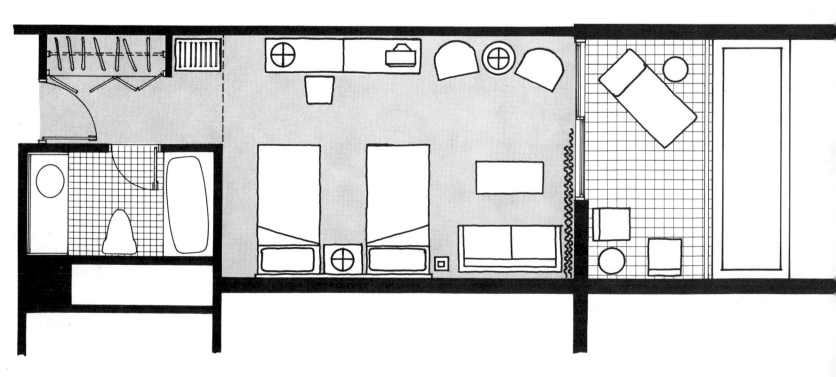

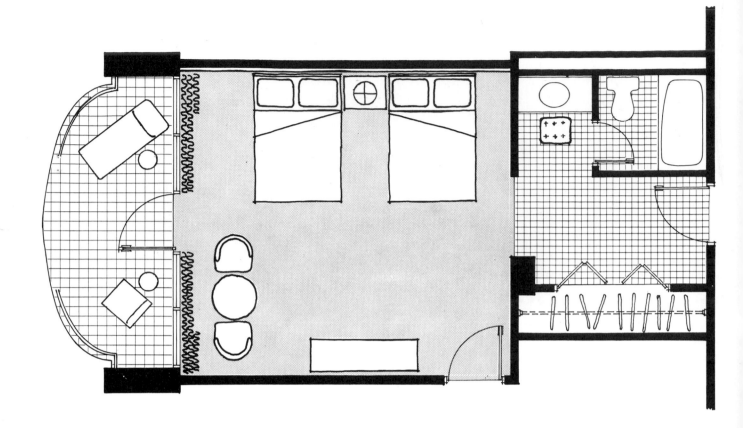

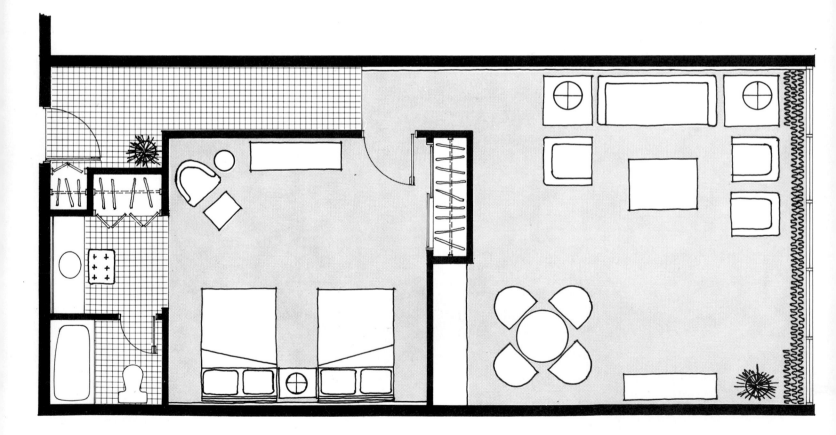

Top: Layout of guest rooms at the Marco Beach Hotel on Marco Island, Florida.

Above: Layout for suite at the Marco Beach Hotel in Marco Island, Florida.

Opposite page top: Typical layout for Ramada Inn guest room.

Opposite page bottom: Typical layout for Ramada Inn suite.

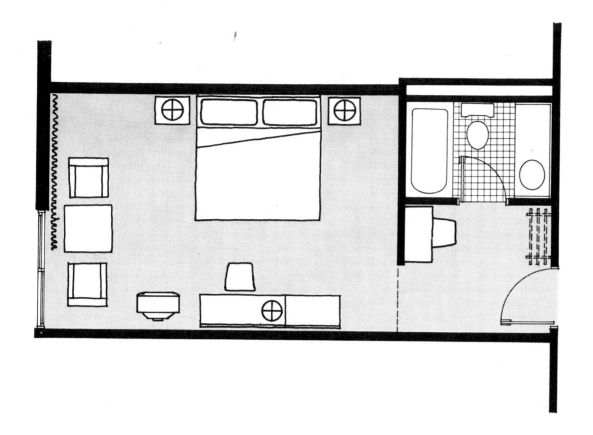

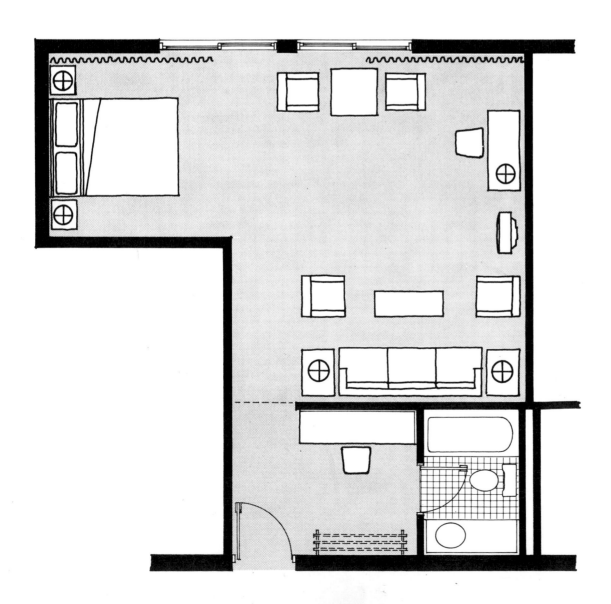

151

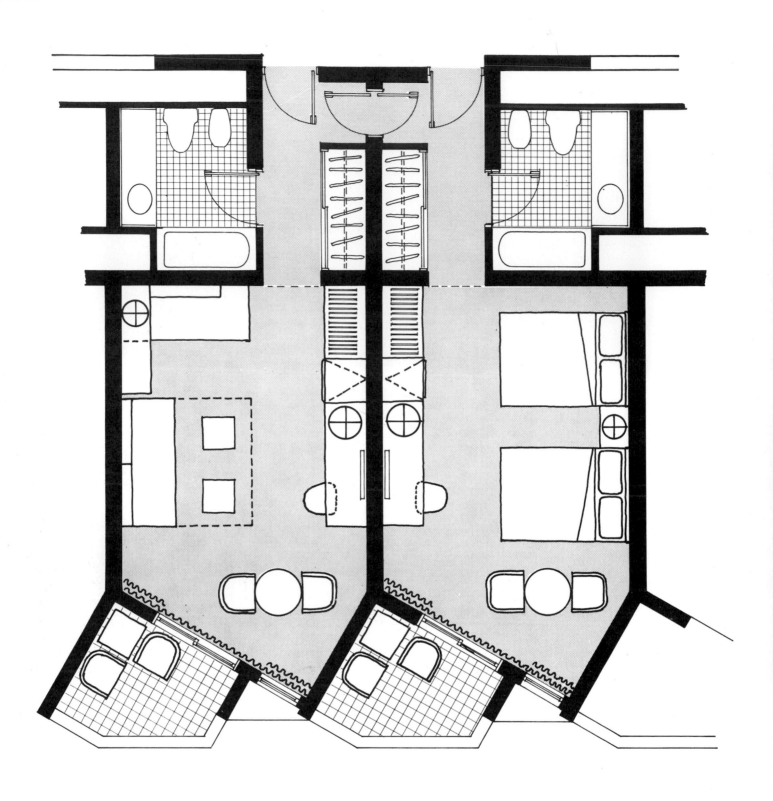

Above: Layout for adjoining rooms at the Karachi Sheraton in Pakistan that can be made into a suite or two separate guest rooms.

Opposite page: Rendering of the Inter-Continental Hotel in Tehran.

154

Opposite page: Rendering of the refreshment lounge in the Inter-Continental in Riyadh, Saudi Arabia.

Above: Rendering of a restaurant in the Hotel Inter-Continental Mecca, a hotel especially designed for Muslim visitors to Mecca.

8. Purchasing and On-Site Supervision

The contract provides the client the option of using our services for purchasing. If our services are accepted, we will charge a fixed percentage of the FOB cost. This will not include freight, duties, or packing. If an item actually costs $100 we may add 10 percent which would be our profit for executing the actual work of purchasing and followthrough. Most interior designers prefer not to be involved because it takes specialized personnel and an organization that can handle the details of purchasing and can, if required, sometimes finance the entire "turnkey" package.

Most of the large management companies either have their own in-house purchasing department or they employ experienced purchasing agents. The latter will accept responsibility for the purchase of the furniture and equipment, including all the back-of-the-house equipment, and will also arrange for shipment, warehousing, and installation.

One of the difficulties in dealing with purchasing agents is that in order to prove their ability to the management company or owner, they seek to purchase as cheaply as possible. But buying cheaper does not necessarily mean buying the same article for less. A purchasing agent might select two chairs that he thinks equally suitable. He will buy the cheaper one rather than the chair specified by the designer who is trying to obtain a total image. There may be even more important differences between the chairs than esthetics. The less expensive chair, because of structural differences, may not have the necessary maintenance factors. We do not object to the employment of a purchasing agent, however, as long as the designer has the final say regarding selection. This should be written into the contract, but even so we find we have to constantly police and monitor the purchasing. And like everything else the concept is no better than the details. For all these reasons we prefer to work with an in-house agent. In any case we carry out all specifications.

After the final approvals we prepare a control book, which becomes the project purchasing specifications. Every design element is recorded with its particular detailed information including sample of material, price, and/or a drawing or photograph of the item. This control book could enable the client's purchasing department to proceed with all the buying for the project. If we are made responsible for the purchasing, the control book is used as the client's checklist. Purchase orders are prepared by us on behalf of the client, forwarded to his authorized personnel for review and approval, and then issued to the supplier. As items are received, they are compared with the specifications in the control book to assure conformity and are inspected for damage prior to acceptance. Upon acceptance and receipt of billing from the supplier, a member of our staff will authorize payment if the item has been found acceptable.

BUDGET

While the interior designer might specify a marble floor or wood partition walls, for example, these things fall within the contractor's budget. All the furniture, furnishings, and equipment—the movable items that are part of an interior—fall within the designer's budget.

If there happens to be a money squeeze toward the end of the project, it is the furnishings that suffer since they are the last thing to be pur-

In almost all cases, furnishings and equipment are obtained through an interior contractor who is responsible, at least in principle, for delivieres and should be obligated by contract to provide substitute materials on schedule if deliveries are delayed. In reality, however, the designer must oversee the contractor at almost every step. Goods are ordered in the client's, not the architect's name, but come to the designer to be reviewed and to be authorized for payment.

Warren Platner, FAIA

A suite in Chicago's Whitehall Hotel.

chased. But that is neither good business nor good sense and is not likely to happen when you are working with the large hotel chains. The interior, as Dale Keller has pointed out, "is like the tip of an iceberg since almost 100 percent of what the guest sees and experiences in a hotel is the interior." And yet, adds Keller, "the interior represents only 10 percent of the project cost."

Of course inflation is one difficulty in keeping to the designer's budget for furniture, furnishings, and equipment. Beds, for instance, might be budgeted this year but they won't be purchased for 3 years, and during that time there may be a 25 percent increase in cost. To take care of such inflated costs we usually add an extra percentage, but generally not more than 15 percent.

Any errors in specification or design can still be corrected if a prototype is made of such repetitious spaces as guest rooms. The seat of a chair might be too high or too low, the corners of a chest too sharp, or perhaps certain materials don't blend as expected—all of which can be changed or modified before any purchase is made. A prototype is also valuable for overseas work where manufacturing companies may not be able to interpret detailed drawings but want to tender on the various components of a project.

ON-SITE SUPERVISION

Wherever necessary, we set up a field office staffed jointly by members of our main office supplemented by local associates. A member of our executive staff is made responsible for the operations of the field office, and when not personally stationed at the field office, he will make periodic visits to assure proper project control. If the project is in a country such as Iran, we might work with a consultant in the Middle East who is familiar with the area. In all hotels, overseas or otherwise, we will have an on-site representative during the last phases of a project—when wallcovering, furnishings, and all the final finishes are being installed.

Close-up of the alcoved passageway in Dublin's Airport Hotel.

9. On the Drawing Board

In spite of numerous predictions of a slowdown in the hotel industry, there are many new hotels on the drawing boards—from spectacular convention hotels to intimate urban hotels, from luxurious resort hotels to simple roadside motels.

An urban trend of the 1970s that has a bearing on the present and future construction of hotels in the U.S. is the renewal of downtown areas going on throughout the country. *Time* discusses the trend in an article called *Downtown Is Looking Up* in the July 5, 1976, issue and comes to the conclusion that all the downtown construction of the 1970s could express a new attitude toward cities.

HOTELS AND THE NEW DOWNTOWN

While the demise of the American city was being bemoaned by many, a quiet revitalization of downtown areas has been going on across the land that may very well prove to be its salvation. Hotels invariably have an important place in these revitalized downtowns which, as *Time* puts it, are giving many U.S. cities a more inviting look as well as a new lease on life. From New York to San Francisco, from Atlanta to Seattle, with many stops in between, downtowns are being transformed into pleasant traffic-free places that mix parks and pedestrian malls with highrise buildings. Tree-studded plazas, fountains, and intimate shopping arcades —"all a recovered legacy from Europe"—are putting U.S. cities in touch with people.

More often than not a hotel is the centerpiece of these revitalized downtowns. Atlanta's Peachtree Center, the brainchild of architect-developer John Portman, boasts two hotels along with five office buildings, a theater, restaurants, and shops. Portman, in fact, has had much to do with giving impetus to the downtown revival just as he has had much to do with the proliferation of the modern atrium hotel on the far corners of the earth. He has rightly been credited with having done more to "change hoteldom than anyone since Conrad Hilton." Portman's hotels, however, are merely part of his larger plan for revitalizing central cities. *Time* quotes him as saying that only downtown can Americans find "the activities that make life significant." And Portman's ideas are contagious.

The cornerstone of San Francisco's Embarcadero Center—another revitalized downtown in which Portman played an important role—is his spectacular Hyatt Regency whose atrium is literally a town square in itself with trees, sidewalk cafes, shops, cocktail lounges, and seating areas. Portman is also the genius behind Detroit's 33-acre Renaissance Center for which a 70-story cylindrical hotel is a striking centerpiece for four 39-story octagonal office towers surrounding it.

Other notable downtown revivals in which hotels are a prominent feature include Kansas City's Crown Center, a felicitous gathering of offices, shops, and the handsome 20-story hotel designed by Harry Weese. Minneapolis's long-range plan for revitalizing downtown has already shown how brilliantly it can work. Automobile-free shopping malls, hotels, office towers, with enclosed pedestrian skyways crisscrossing all, have proven to be the successful ingredients of a vital downtown. West-

All buildings do not need windows. They are unnecessary for department stores, hotels, shopping centers, telephone exchanges theatres, warehouses, and the like. So what would happen if in such instances, conventional structures were replaced by Mayan pyramids covered with greenery? With parking spaces hidden underground? Answer and solution: you'd have hillsides and slopes providing pleasant views for people living in apartment buildings. If I had the opportunity to translate the theory into reality, I would start with "a sort of invisible shopping center," but at this point I can only hope that some day, an enterprising developer will say "why not?" and give the go-ahead.

George Nelson, FAIA, FIDSA

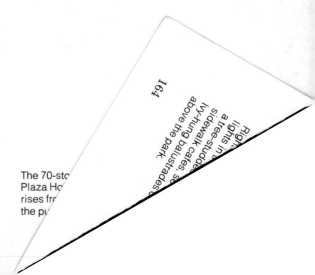

164

The 70-sto
Plaza H[...]
rises fr[...]
the p[...]

Right[...] in[...]
sidewalk cafes [...]
a tree-studde[...]
IVy-hung balustrades[...]
above the par[...]

Above: The U.N. Plaza Hotel in New York rises
behind the United Nations General Assembly
Building.

Right: The 17-floor high atrium lit from glass sky-
the Hyatt Regency San Francisco is like
urban park. It includes fountains,
ating areas, shops, sculpture.
of the guest floors rise

lake Mall in Seattle, designed by architect Aldo Giurgola, consists of a plaza-flanked multitiered structure containing a hotel, shops, restaurants, movie theaters, and a terminal for the city's monorail. In Dallas a new retail and cultural complex with a direct rapid-rail link to the Dallas–Fort Worth Airport features a Hyatt hotel. And there are more examples of revitalized downtown areas in Denver, Cleveland, St. Louis, Milwaukee, to name but a few.

Attention was also called in the *Time* article to another product of city center renewal: the changing shape of the skyscraper. Replacing the monotonous slab of the 1960s is "a completely new series of high-rise shapes and configurations: ribbed, faceted, angled, notched and cylindrical." And often these newly shaped towers house a hotel in whole or in part. Portman's Peachtree Plaza Hotel in Atlanta occupies the entire 70-story bronze-glass-clad cylindrical tower he designed for it. One United Nations Plaza in New York—a glittering glass structure designed by architects Roche/Dinkeloo that seems to change shape with the changing light—devotes the top 13 of its 39 stories to the elegant United Nations Plaza Hotel. Water Tower Place, a 74-story commercial-retail-residential complex in Chicago, although not so oddly shaped, has the famed Ritz-Carlton Hotel as a 22-floor tenant.

And so "with all their pathologies," as Roland Gelatt put it in the August 21, 1976, *Saturday Review*, "cities—at least some cities—are beginning to look good again." And, as classic components of the good city life, so are some hotels.

IN THE FUTURE

As for the more distant future, transportation and technological advances will probably have the greatest influence on hotels and their design as they have in the past. Just as the hotel of the 19th century was controlled by transportation, so is the hotel of the 20th century, and so, in all probability, will be the hotel of the 21st century. Americans have long realized that travel is the hotel's raison d'etre—a haven for both tourists and business people. The railroads sired the railroad hotel, the automobile sired the motel, the airlines sired the airport hotel, and the space capsule may well sire the satellite hotel!

Today's hotels are not so different from the People's Palaces of the 19th century, except in technological details, size, and matters of taste. The innkeeper of 100 years ago might have tried to imagine the hotel of today just as we might imagine a hotel spinning in space or under the sea.

The American hotel has always been in the vanguard as far as innovations go. Boston's Tremont of 1829 ushered in gaslight and water closets; New York's Astor House installed the first passenger elevator in 1859; and New York's Hotel Everett installed electric lights early in 1882. And technological advances will certainly have a great influence on the design of hotels in the future. It is possible to envision a totally automated, self-service hotel in which the guest never has contact with the hotel personnel. It is more comforting to think, however, that hotels will continue to be what psychologist Dr. James Bond called them in 1966, "one of the last bulwarks against depersonalization."

In the 19th century the English journalist George Augustus Sala noted that "the American hotel is to an English hotel what an elephant is to a periwinkle." That is no longer true. The American hotel in the 20th century ushered in automation and the atrium and exported the idea of the modern American hotel to the far corners of the globe. And in spite of rising costs and staffing problems, the modern American hotel is bound to proliferate into even more remote areas in the 21st century. There are still hotels to build in the Middle East, while the next boom will probably be in Africa. The American custom of holding conventions is becoming ever-more popular and the ambition of some of the world's lesser cities to have prestige hotels has by no means been satisfied. Herman Kahn, a

Meanwhile, the advance of technology has presented the architect with a vast array of new metallic alloys and new plastics, with new structural materials like prestressed concrete, with new large-scale elements useful for modular designs, and with new mechanical devices that add to the total cost of the structure, as well as the upkeep. On the assumption that mechanical progress is itself more important than human purposes, the architect has felt, it would seem, almost a moral obligation to use all these materials and methods, if only to maintain his status as a creative designer. In this respect, the architect finds himself in almost the same unfortunate position as the physician, overwhelmed by the enormous number of new antibiotics and other drugs that are thrust on the market by the great pharmaceutical organizations, and often unable to follow through one remedy before a new one is thrust on him.

Louis Mumford

trained physicist who specializes in predicting the world's future, told in the August 9, 1976, issue of *New York* magazine that the four-day weekend will revolutionize hotels in the 21st century. That, explains Kahn, is because Americans will spend a considerably larger part of their income on diverse "experiences"—travel and epicurean delights—than on basic material requirements.

Certainly the prepackaged hotel guest room and bathroom that can be hoisted into place complete with all their furnishing as has been done in Florida's Disney World will be part of the future of hotel design; disposable items such as paper sheets and pillow cases will probably be used within the next 10 years since service costs along with all other costs will continue to escalate.

When the elegant Astor House opened in New York in the 1830s, guests paid $3 a week for room and board. Today a single room in that city's more elegant hotels can cost little short of $100 a night without even a cup of coffee. Hotels have been becoming ever-more splendid as well as ever-more expensive since the 19th century when the acerbic Mrs. Trollope reported that the City Hotel in Baltimore "is said to be the most splendid in the union, and it is certainly splendid enough for a people more luxurious than the citizens of the republic appear yet to be."

In any case tomorrow's hotel designer, like today's hotel designer, will probably have to be able to understand his client and his needs. He will have to understand how design can influence the behavior of people using a particular space. He will need even more diversified and professional skill than he does today. He will need talent and sensitivity just as he always has. In the 19th century New Yorker Abraham Oakley Hall called Isaiah Rogers' St. Charles Hotel in New Orleans "a place for creature comforts, a college for the study of human nature; and an exchange for money and appetite." So is today's successful hotel and so probably will be tomorrow's. It may have been a 19th-century American formula but it still works and probably will in the 21st century.

"Railway termini and hotels are to the nineteenth century what monasteries and cathedrals were to the thirteenth century," stated the editors of *Building News* in 1875. "They are truly the only really representative buildings we possess...."

Below: Model of the Marriott Hotel in Cairo is built around an old palace.

Opposite page top: Proposed hotel for Kish, an island in the Persian Gulf that the Iranian shah wishes to make into a resort complex with hotels, housing, and casinos.

Opposite page bottom: Villars La Rocha, a proposed hotel for Switzerland.

PEACHTREE PLAZA HOTEL IN ATLANTA, GEORGIA

One of the most recent evolutions of the great atrium space that John Portland pioneered in the Hyatt Regency Atlanta and which changed the whole theory of hotel design.

Above left and right: Night-time and daytime views of the main skylit space from which the tower rises. Boat-shaped islands between the columns serve as places to have a drink or just view the drama.

Right: The top level is a circular cocktail lounge with a revolving platform. The dining level also revolves. Island-like structures are at the restaurant's intermediate level.

Opposite page: Bridges connect the tower to the rest of the building.

10. Standards, Schedules, and Contracts

This chapter consists of a series of organizational lists, contracts, and forms that the designer needs to structure his day-to-day work.

SHERATON'S INTERIOR DESIGN QUALITY STANDARDS

1. General

Samples of all items should be fabricated, tested (simulating actual conditions), and approved by Sheraton prior to starting production. Manufacturers shall give a minimum guarantee of one year for all furnishings against defects in materials and workmanship.

All fabric and carpet samples submitted for approval must be accompanied by detailed specifications, revealing construction and fiber content.

All soft goods—carpet, draperies, bedspreads and upholstery—should be flame rated and treated for flame resistance.

All wall coverings and all interior finish materials shall meet the local codes pertaining to flame spread.

2. Furniture

A. General

Requirements

1. Heavy-duty, first-quality workmanship and materials.
2. No particle board to be used.
3. Chairs to have heavy bracing.
4. All movable furniture to have nylon (not metal) screw-in glides.
5. All edges to be hardwood, not plastic laminate.
6. All drawers to have ball bearing extension glides and stops.
7. Foam rubber for upholstery should be dense quality and receive cotton padding and muslim cover.
8. Provide pianos.
9. Provide furniture and furnishings for offices and employees cafeteria.
10. Provide furniture and furnishings for powder rooms.
11. Provide beach furniture (lounges, umbrellas, life guard stand, waste receptacles, etc.).
12. Outdoor furniture to be rust-proof, heavy duty, and not prone to sun lotion stains.
13. Provide all game furniture for game room including billiard, table tennis, and card tables.

Comments

Plexiglas and most moulded plastic furniture shows scratches badly, especially with a shiny finish.

B. Guest Rooms

Requirements

1. A few extra pieces of all guest room furniture to be provided for reserve.

The problems and frustrations involved in obtaining equipment and furniture and in dealing with the furniture industry are legion: notice comes without warning—or opportunity for recourse —that deliveries will be delayed 10 weeks and prices raised 10 percent. Period.

Warren Platner, FAIA

Dining area in a suite at the Hyatt Regency Hong Kong, a business, resort, and tourist hotel.

2. Guest room chest drawers to have plastic laminate bottoms.

3. Guest room night tables to include radio, light controls, wake-up system, etc.

4. Guest room case goods to have plastic laminate top (as always on both sides to avoid warping).

5. All walls to have vinyl wall covering or approved equal.

6. Guest room coffee tables to have plastic laminate or other as practical top.

7. Quality of box spring and mattresses to conform to Sheraton standards [as defined in attachment A which must be obtained from Sheraton].

8. Box springs not to be exposed to view when bedspread is removed.

9. Bed frames to have nylon rollers (or glides on tiles).

Comments

Nonupholstered arms are practical for guestroom lounge chairs.

C. Restaurants

Requirements

1. Provide special food carts as required.

2. See [attachment B which must be obtained from Sheraton for] guideline dimensions for service stands, captain's stand, waiter's carts, music stands, etc. (These sketches are not meant to suggest designs.)

3. For restaurant table sizes [see attachment C which must be obtained from Sheraton].

4. Restaurant table tops which are intended for table cloth only must be ³/₄″ (20 mm) marine plywood with metal band and have foam-vinyl cover permanently attached to top. All table bases to be heavy type with adjustable glides.

5. Provide a few reserve chairs and tables for restaurant.

6. Provide high and youth seats chairs for restaurants.

7. Planter to have liner which allows excess water to settle at bottom without "souring" the earth and which is leakproof.

D. Banquet Facilities

Requirements

1. Ballroom and meeting room chairs to be stackable.

2. Provide lecterns (table and standing) for ballroom.

3. Provide movable stage platforms.

4. Provide movable dance floor.

E. Lobby

Requirements

1. Brochure rack in lobby to contain space for 45 different folders of hotels. Each folder is 4 in. (10 cm) x 9 in. (23 cm). To be designed so that it can be easily expanded at a later date.

2. Provide bulletin board in main lobby near front desk with removable letters for changing announcements.

3. Portable poster display units for public spaces to accommodate 2 posters 28 in. (71 cm) x 40 in. (102 cm). Total height about 48 in. (112 cm).

4. Each elevator to have two frames for 16 x 19¹/₂ in. (40 x 50 cm) posters. The same size frames should be used on elevator landings and where required by Sheraton.

F. Upholstery Fabric

Requirements

1. All fabrics to be scotchguarded (or zepel) and preshrunk (shrinkage factor to be less than 2 percent).

2. All vinyl upholstery to be of breathable kind, have stretch backing, and be easily washable.

3. Only heavy-duty textured knitted fabrics can be accepted.

4. Supply extra yardage of all custom-made fabrics.

Comments

1. Most ideal is wool or a wool synthetic combination (70 percent wool, 30 percent synthetic) tightly woven.

2. Cotton or rayon do not stand up well and are extremely difficult to keep clean.

3. One hundred percent nylon fabric has a tendency to retain soil.

4. Good back coating (latex or similar) important, for loosely woven fabrics in particular.

5. Do not use vinyl in hot climate outdoors or in un-air conditioned spaces.

6. Heavy canvas is a good outdoor fabric.

7. Terry cloth cover over pool lounge mattresses are advantageous.

G. Drapery

Requirements

1. Normal fullness to be 100–150 percent depending on type of fabric.

2. Guest room drapery to have separate blackout lining. (Separate track.)

3. Use batons rather than cord pull mechanism for guest rooms—unless fabric is very fragile.

4. Provide at least 5 percent each color for reserve of guest room drapery.

5. Do not use fiberglass.

6. Sample wash or dry clean.

7. All fabrics to be scotchguarded and preshrunk.

8. Supply extra yardage of all custom-made fabrics.

9. All hems to be weighted.

10. Curtain tracks to be heavy duty, at least 4 in. (10 cm) on center when two tracks are used.

11. All public room drapery must be flameproofed.

Comments

1. If attached lining must be used, be sure shrinking factor of both fabrics is the same.

2. Piece dyed fabrics (as opposed to yarn dyed) have a tendency to fade when exposed to strong sun.

H. Bedspreads

Requirements

1. Pillow has to fit under bedspread.

2. To be easily washable or dry cleanable (depending on availability of either facility).

3. Test wash or dry clean.

4. To be preshrunk.

5. Ten percent of each color and size to be ordered as reserve.

I. Carpet

Requirements

1. All carpets (with the exception of some suites) to be multicolored or patterned.

2. Large area rugs to be recessed, preshrunk.

3. Order a minimum of 5 percent overage for each color, 10 percent if custom patterns are used.

4. Underlay to be sponge, rubber or foam, weight 50–56 oz (1.5–1.7 liters) per square yard.

5. Where static electricity is a problem, a stainless steel fiber should be woven into the carpet.

6. Outdoor carpets to be acrylic or polypropylene with special outdoor backing.

7. Provide two pieces of carpet for each elevator.

8. For guideline carpet specifications (see following chart).

Comments

Wool and synthetic (70 percent wool, 30 percent preferably acrylic) is the best combination in a dense tufted or knitted woven through the back loop or cut pile.

The minimum standards for guest rooms are as follows:

Tufted, cut pile
70 percent acrylic, 30 percent modacrylic
$3/16$ gauge, 8 row
$9/10$ pile height
3 ply yarn, 35 ounce face weight
71 ounce total weight
Primary backing jute
Secondary backing jute

The minimum standards for corridors are as follows:

Tufted
$5/32$ gauge
Pile height .306
100 percent twist set nylon
2 ply yarn, 35 ounce face weight
84 ounce total weight
Primary backing jute
Secondary backing jute

The minimum standards for public spaces are as follows:

10 row
250 pile high
252 pitch
80 percent wool, 20 percent nylon
36 ounce face weight
Primary backing jute
Secondary backing jute

J. Lighting Fixtures

1. All lamps to have heavy weighted bases.

2. All table lamps to have base switches and one-way sockets.

3. Guest room nighttable fixtures must have separate light sources and switch for each bed at lamp base.

K. Wall Covering

Vinyl to be cloth backed, minimum weight of $12^{1}/_{2}$ oz (0.3 liters) for guest room, 25 oz (0.7 liters) for public spaces.

L. Uniforms

Fabric to be noniron drip-dry (preshrunk).

M. Accessories

1. Provide table lamps in all restaurants, glass shades to be extra thick.

2. Special china for specialty restaurant and special utensils to be selected in coordination with Sheraton Food and Beverage Management.

3. Provide sand urns at each elevator landing.

4. Provide ashtrays and flower vases for all restaurants but not the ballroom or function rooms. (Already included in equipment budget.)

N. Mattress (Sheraton Crestline)

Innerspring Mattress

1. Sizes, coil counts, and gauges:

76 x 80	396 coil	18 x 24	13 gauge	9 gauge border wire
5/0 x 80	360 coil	15 x 24	13 gauge	9 gauge border wire
4/6 x 75	308 coil	14 x 22	13 gauge	9 gauge border wire
4/6 x 80	336 coil	14 x 24	13 gauge	9 gauge border wire
3/3 x 75	198 coil	9 x 22	13 gauge	9 gauge border wire
3/3 x 80	216 coil	2 x 24	13 gauge	9 gauge border wire

2. The innerspring unit is an all-wire special spring unit constructed of transverse rows of 13 gauge, semicylindrical offset coils, 5 in. (13 cm) high with a five turn configuration which is connected by 17 gauge helical at right angles to the long axis of the unit.

The flat offset sides of the coil joined by the helical prevent any possibility of lateral slippage of the coil. In addition, the hinging action resulting from the offset helical connection allows for proper body support combined with surface comfort conformity. All coils are not less than .092 in. (.2 cm) diameter high-carbon steel spring wire. The helicals are not less than .054 in. (.14 cm) diameter high-carbon steel spring wire. Each offset coil is joined by the helical with a 4 or 5 turn tie per offset bar. All helical ends are trimmed and turned and form a smooth rounded termination.

A 9 gauge border wire which has a diameter of .1483 in. (.35 cm) is secured to the outer row of coils by means of 17 gauge helical which attaches with a minimum of three turns. The border wire provides the support framework for seating usage and is butt-welded at the ends.

3. The unit is twice tempered. Each coil is individually and electronically heat tempered at a minimum temperature of 450° F. After completing the assembly, the entire unit is oven tempered for stress relief at 450° F for a minimum cycle of 20 minutes. The tensile strengths of the following components are:

a. Offset coils: 215,000 to 260,000 PSI.

b. Helicals: 240,000 to 280,000 PSI.

c. Borders: 185,000 to 210,000 PSI.

4. The insulation and upholstery is as follows:

a. Primary insulator. A spun-bonded polypropylene pad or a wire insulator pad is placed and fastened to each side of the offset innerspring unit. The insulator wires shall contain 20 gauge oil tempered wire strands, 1¹/₄ in. (3 cm) spacing between wires and shall be the same size as the innerspring unit.

b. Secondary insulator. A 2³/₄–3 oz (80–90 mliters) per square foot unit size sisal pad or oversize ¹/₄ in. (.6 cm) polyurethane pad [¹/₃ lb (.13 kg) density] or approved alternate is placed on each side over the innerspring unit. Each pad is fastened at six primary distinct points.

c. The upholstery layers are as follows:

Cotton layer felt, precompressed, weighing a minimum of 4 ¹/₈ oz. (.14 liters) per square foot.

Polyurethane topper pad of ¹/₃ lb (.13 kg) density, ¹/₄ in. (.6 cm) thick.

Surface. The cover is multineedle quilted to a ³/₈ in. (1 cm) polyurethane pad of 1.3 lb (.6 kg) density.

5. Covering material. The ticking is a hotel weight woven stripe fabric or approved alternate.

6. Flanging and filling operation. The flange consists of a 5 in. (12.7 cm) wide strip of flame-retardant fabric, machine sewn ¾ in. (1.9 cm) inside the outer hem of the top and bottom ticking panels. The entire insulation and upholstery filling is securely anchored to the edge of the unit in the form of a snug inner-roll by fastening the flanging material to each and every perimeter coil with metal rings. The flanging process reinforces the edges and keeps the filling material from shifting.

7. Finishing. The mattress is bench built with the cover sewn to the boxing after the filling operation. A variegated tape is used in closing the mattress. The mattress shall be well finished, clean, free from defects and shall meet all flammability standards.

8. Boxing. Borders are made of the specified ticking and are in one piece with the ends securely sewn to each other. The border is quilted by machine, using padding weighing at least 3 oz (85 grams) per running yard.

Foundation Unit

1. The foundation unit is a unique back-support system. It is a geometrically formed unit that is constructed of a series of 8½ gauge levers and torsion bars designed to provide a specific load deflection characteristic.

2. This unit is designed with specialized edge support units, varying in number by the size of the foundation. This unit is also programmed so that additional support units are placed in the center third of the construction. All members are assembled together with formed 20 gauge cold rolled clip.

An 8½ gauge border wire is secured to the perimeter of the unit by means of a 20 gauge cold rolled clip.

Sizes and counts:

52½ x 74	32 edge support members	16 center support members
52½ x 79	32 edge support members	20 center support members
37½ x 74	28 edge support members	10 center support members
37½ x 79	28 edge support members	12 center support members
59½ x 79	34 edge support members	24 center support members

The above dimensions include a tolerance of + ½ in. (1.3 cm).

3. Frame. The box spring frame is constructed of seasoned or kiln dried spruce or its equivalent and is warp resistant.

Each row of the intermediate springs rests on a supporting cross slat.

The frame is square and flat with 8 cross slats plus the ends. All corners are cut with approximately 3 in. (7.6 cm) radius and the bottom edges are chamfered with a ⅛ in. (.3 cm) bevel on the entire perimeter. All frames, except twin size, have center support rail. All end and side rails are reinforced with stiffeners to add to the rigidity of the frame. All wood stock is ⅝ in. (1.6 cm) plus a 1/16 in. (1.5 cm) tolerance.

2 end rails	2½ in. (6.3 cm) wide
2 end stiffeners	¾ in. (1.9 cm) to 1⅛ in. (2.8 cm) wide
1 center rail	1½ in. (3.8 cm) wide
2 side rails	2½ in. (6.3 cm) wide
2 side fillers	1¼ in. (3.1 cm) wide
4 cross slats	1½ in. (3.8 cm) wide
4 cross slats	2½ in. (6.3 cm) wide

The frame is securely nailed and either comes braced on one corner or glued on four corners.

4. The insulation and filling is as follows:

a. Primary. A full unit-size wire mesh or spun-bonded polypropylene insulator pad is placed over the foundation unit.

b.   Secondary. A 2½ oz (70 mliters) per square foot sisal pad or approved alternate is placed over the top of the primary insulator; edges of the sisal pad or alternate are rolled over box springs border wire.

c.   Upholstery layers. A 2¾ oz (80 mliters) per square foot cotton felt layer or approved alternate is placed over the sisal pad and around the edge wire. The corners of the box spring are held out by corner support modules so that the unit tailors smooth and straight.

5.   Covering material. The ticking is to match that specified for the mattress.

6.   Dust cover. The bottom of the box spring is enclosed by sheeting which is stapled to the perimeter of the wood frame.

7.   Boxing. Borders are made of the specified ticking and are in one piece with ends securely sewn to each other.

O. Standard Table Sizes

Location	Persons		Size
Coffee shop	2		75 x 60 cm
	4		75 x 75 cm
	4		75 x 120 cm
	4	Ø	92 cm
Restaurant	2		85 x 75 cm
	4		85 x 85 cm
	4		85 x 120 cm
	4	Ø	110 cm
	4–6	Ø	120 cm (85 x 85 cm)
Main dining	2	Ø	80 cm
Resort hotel	2–4		75 x 75 cm
	4		75 x 120 cm
Banquet	6		75 x 180 cm
	3		37.5 x 180 cm (schoolroom)
	4	Ø	120 cm
	6–8	Ø	150 cm
	10–12	Ø	180 cm
	Buffet		180 half round

Special tables to set up buffet, meeting, etc.

	Special		270 cm 5/5th
Room service	4	Ø	100 cm
Trays	Coffee shop	Ø	50 cm antislip
	Breakfast/dining		45 x 60 cm
	Banquet		90 cm oval antislip (to fit five plates 28 cm)
	Bar	Ø	35 cm antislip
	Employees' cafeteria		30 x 45 cm

MISCELLANEOUS DESIGN

A. Graphics

1.   Basic image

a.   Design of a logo (typographic treatment of hotel's name).

b.   Selection of a set of colors.

c.   Selection of an alphabet and numerals to be used consistently throughout the hotel.

2. Basic materials (stationery): executive/regular.

a. First page regular and/or air mail weight.

b. Second pages regular and/or air mail weight.

c. Regular and air mail envelopes.

d. Memo note paper.

e. Compliments slips.

f. Labels.

g. Credit cards and credit card holders.

h. Application forms.

i. Guest comment slips.

j. Scratch pads.

k. Service directory.

l. Temporary signboards.

m. Work in progress advertisement.

n. General brochure and rate card.

o. Press kit.

3. General hotel graphics

a. Architectural signs.

b. Interior signs (lobby desks, elevators, mail boxes, room numbers, rest rooms, travel and tour signs, shop signs, etc.).

c. Interior and exterior traffic and directional signs.

d. Staff badges.

e. Limousine.

f. Luggage tag and sticker.

g. Cloak room tag.

h. Guest ID card.

i. Key tag.

j. Message blank.

k. Guest note pad.

4. Guest Room Items

a. Telephone directory cover.

b. Ballpoint pen.

c. Do Not Disturb sign.

d. Clean Up Room sign.

e. Breakfast menu.

f. Room service menu.

g. Stationery kit—first pages, envelopes, ladies note paper and envelopes, guest information folder.

h. Post card (air mail).

i. Matches.

j. Laundry and dry cleaning list.

k. Laundry bag and/or box.

l. Shirt bag.

m. Shoe cloth.

n. Sterilized bands for W.C. (toilets).

o. Drinking glass sterilized bag.

p. Soap wrapper.

q. Doorknob menus.

r. Beach bags.

s. Sewing kit.

t. Linen: bath linen (towels), hand towel, bathmat, shower curtain, bed linen, blankets.

5. Restaurant and bar items

a. Menus designed to match the theme and decor of each bar and restaurant.

b. Drink lists as above.

c. Wine lists as above.

d. Cocktail stirrer.

e. Sugar wrappers, cube and/or granulated.

f. Silverware.

g. Coasters.

h. Placements.

i. Reservation cards.

j. Guest and restaurant bill forms.

k. Function room menu covers and inserts.

l. Drinking straw wrappers.

m. Match designs for each restaurant/bar.

n. Cake/sandwich box.

B. China, Silver, Crystal

1. China, main restaurant, complete service

a. Plates—dinner, dessert, bread and butter, soup.

b. Coffee cup and saucer.

c. Bouillon cup.

d. Oval vegetable dish.

e. Grapefruit, oatmeal dish.

f. Double egg cup.

g. Demitasse and turkish coffee cup and saucer.

h. Salad bowl.

i. Creamer: 2, 4, and 6 oz.

j. Tea pot and coffee pot for both single portion and double portion.

k. Cover for above pot.

l. Water pot single portion and cover.

m. Coffee shop bouillon cup, unhandled.

n. Service plates (china/glass/special).

o. Ashtrays (china, glass, special).

p. Table lamps.

2. Coffee Shop, complete service

a. Same as above.

b. Service plates.

c. Ashtrays.

d. Table lamps.

3. Crystal: all restaurants and bars

a. All glassware desired with crest or emblem.

b. Iced tea, 12 oz.

c. Water goblet, 14 oz.

d. Water servier, 1 quart (for bar services).

e. Soda and milk shake glass.

f. Cocktail glasses, 4½, 6, 9, 10, 12, and 14 oz.

g. Beer goblet, 10 oz.

h. Brandy glass, 13 oz.

i. Special glass.

C. Uniforms

1. Exterior

a. Doorman, summer/winter.

b. Chauffeur, summer/winter.

c. Pool attendants.

2. Interior (front office and lobby area)

a. Clerk (man/women).

b. Information clerk (man/woman).

c. Bell captain.

d. Bellman/elevator starter.

e. Page boy.

f. Lobby porter.

3. Coffee Shop

a. Hostess.

b. Head waiter.

c. Captain.

d. Waiter (man/woman).

e. Busboy.

4. Specialty restaurant/grill room

a. (Hostess).

b. Head waiter, maitre d'.

c. Captain.

d. Waiter (man/woman).

e. Busboy.

f. Sommelier.

5. Main Restaurant

a. (Hostess).

b. Head waiter (maitre d', daytime/nighttime).

c. Assistant head waiter (daytime/nighttime).

d. Captain (daytime/nighttime).

e. Waiter.

f. Busboy.

g. Sommelier.

6. Main Bar

a. (Hostess).

b. Captain.

c. Bar waiter.

d. Bartender (both special and in all areas).

7. Banquet/room service

a. Head waiter.

b. Assistant head waiter.

c. Waiter.

d. Busboy.

8. Floor

a. Supervisor (man/woman).

b. Maids' room (daytime/nighttime).

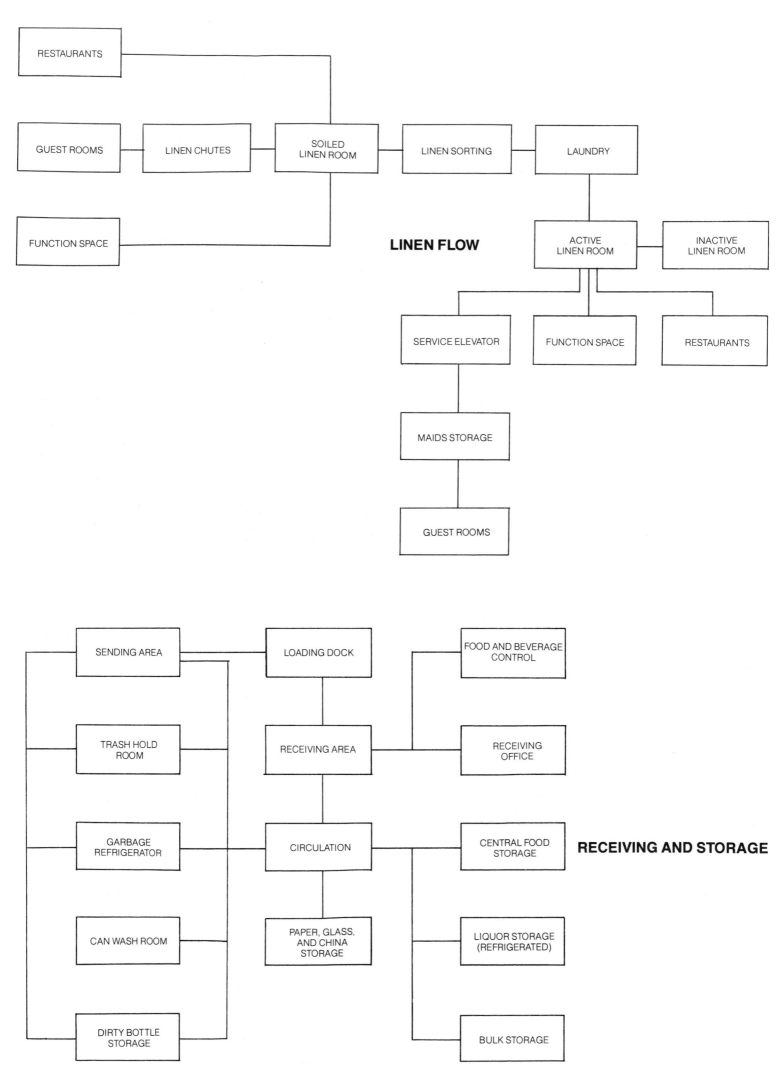

LINEN FLOW

RECEIVING AND STORAGE

180

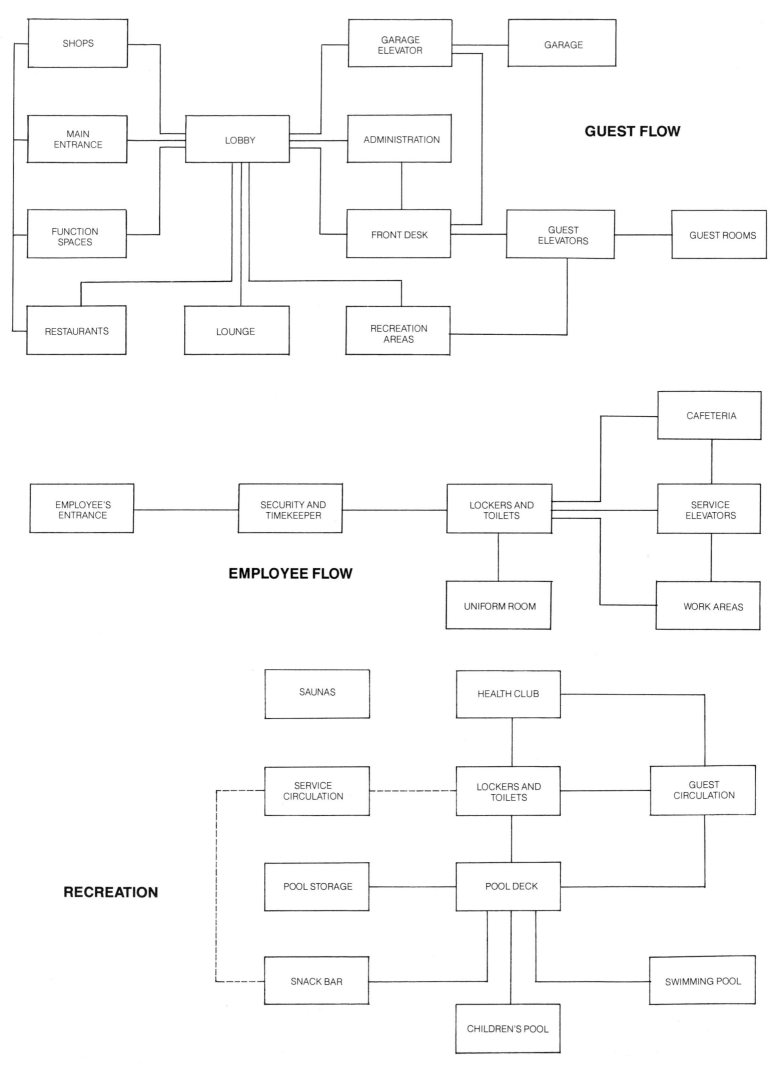

GUEST FLOW

SHOPS

GARAGE ELEVATOR

GARAGE

MAIN ENTRANCE

LOBBY

ADMINISTRATION

FUNCTION SPACES

FRONT DESK

GUEST ELEVATORS

GUEST ROOMS

RESTAURANTS

LOUNGE

RECREATION AREAS

EMPLOYEE FLOW

CAFETERIA

EMPLOYEE'S ENTRANCE

SECURITY AND TIMEKEEPER

LOCKERS AND TOILETS

SERVICE ELEVATORS

UNIFORM ROOM

WORK AREAS

RECREATION

SAUNAS

HEALTH CLUB

SERVICE CIRCULATION

LOCKERS AND TOILETS

GUEST CIRCULATION

POOL STORAGE

POOL DECK

SNACK BAR

SWIMMING POOL

CHILDREN'S POOL

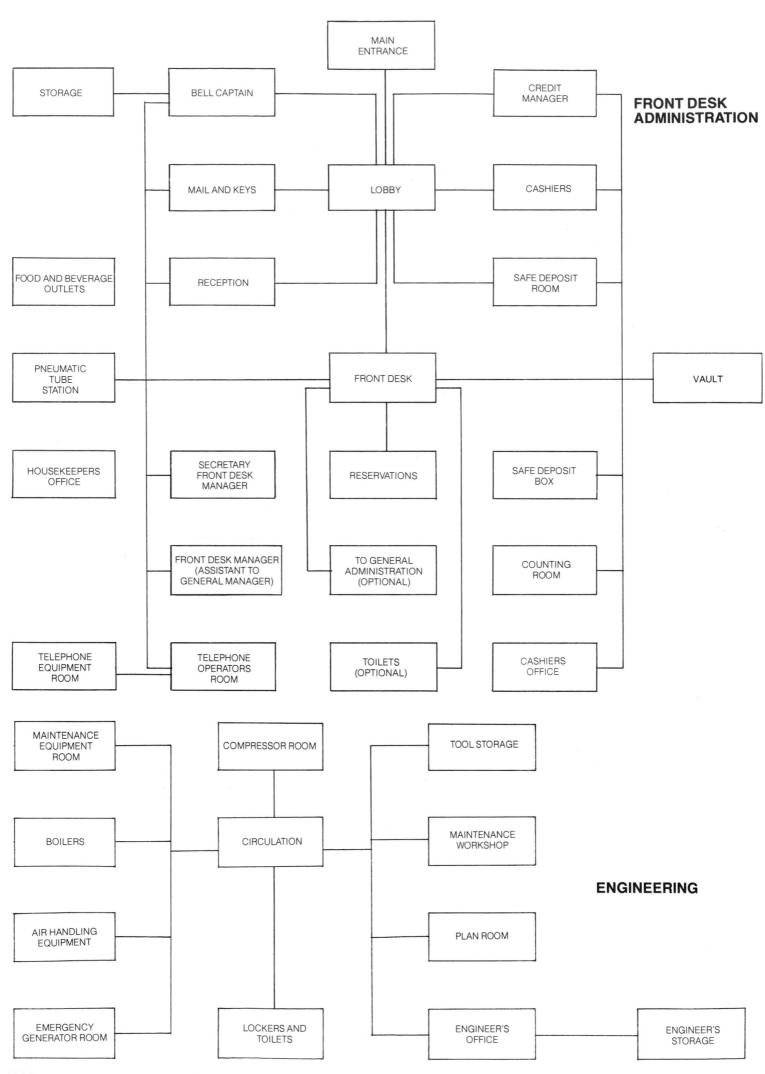

FRONT DESK ADMINISTRATION

ENGINEERING

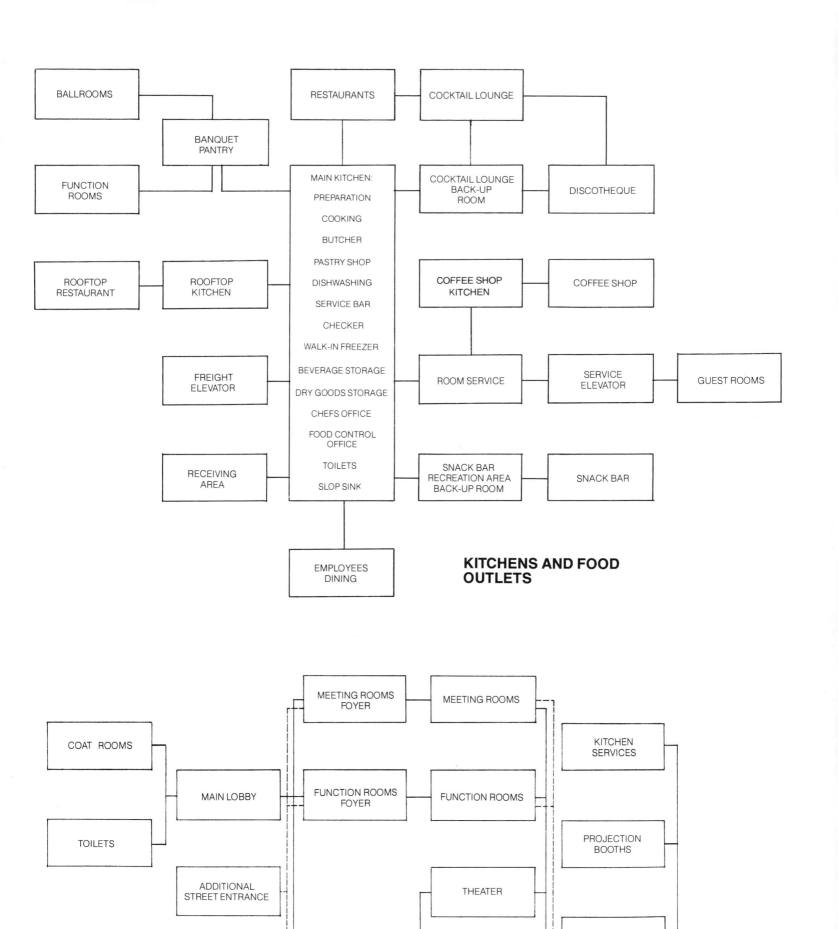

KITCHENS AND FOOD OUTLETS

BALLROOMS

BANQUET PANTRY

FUNCTION ROOMS

RESTAURANTS

COCKTAIL LOUNGE

COCKTAIL LOUNGE BACK-UP ROOM

DISCOTHEQUE

MAIN KITCHEN:
PREPARATION
COOKING
BUTCHER
PASTRY SHOP
DISHWASHING
SERVICE BAR
CHECKER
WALK-IN FREEZER
BEVERAGE STORAGE
DRY GOODS STORAGE
CHEFS OFFICE
FOOD CONTROL OFFICE
TOILETS
SLOP SINK

ROOFTOP RESTAURANT

ROOFTOP KITCHEN

COFFEE SHOP KITCHEN

COFFEE SHOP

FREIGHT ELEVATOR

ROOM SERVICE

SERVICE ELEVATOR

GUEST ROOMS

RECEIVING AREA

SNACK BAR RECREATION AREA BACK-UP ROOM

SNACK BAR

EMPLOYEES DINING

FUNCTION AREAS

COAT ROOMS

TOILETS

MAIN LOBBY

ADDITIONAL STREET ENTRANCE

MEETING ROOMS FOYER

MEETING ROOMS

FUNCTION ROOMS FOYER

FUNCTION ROOMS

KITCHEN SERVICES

PROJECTION BOOTHS

TRANSLATION BOOTHS

THEATER

BALLROOM FOYER

EXHIBITION SPACE

SERVICE

BALLROOM

BALLROOM FOYER

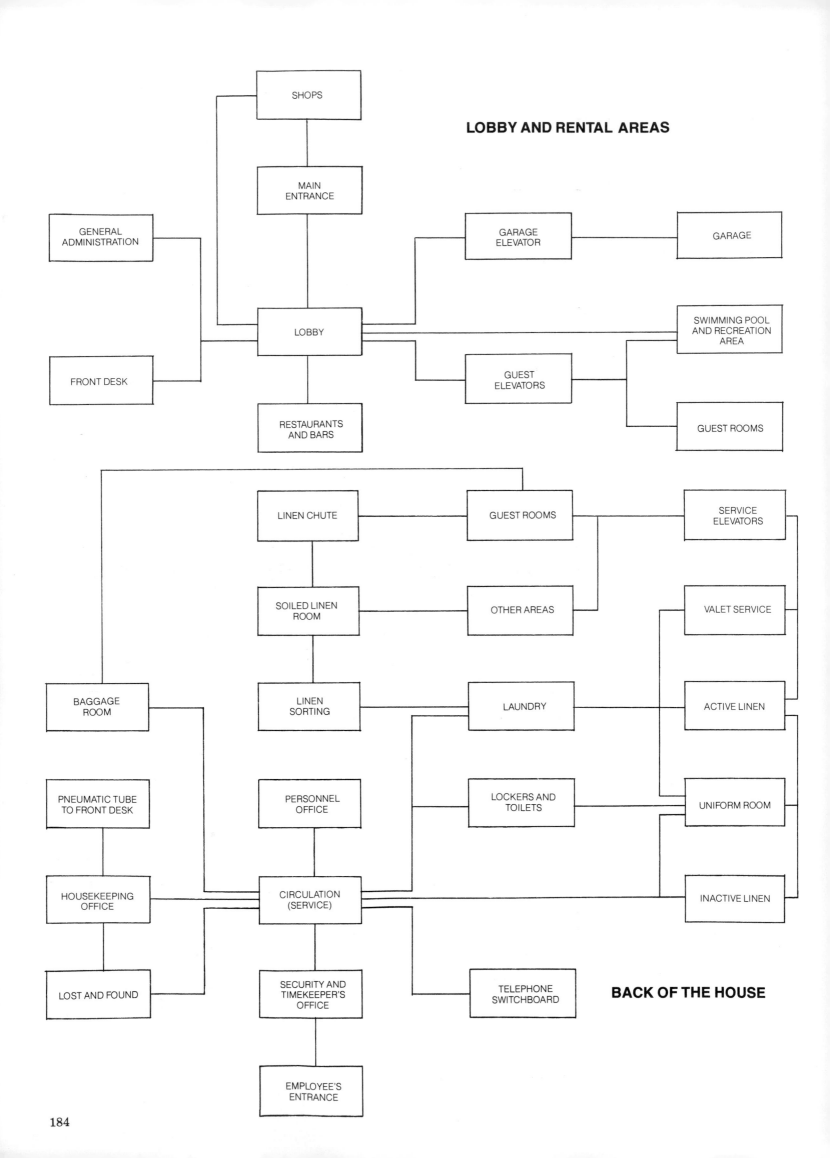

LOBBY AND RENTAL AREAS

SHOPS

MAIN ENTRANCE

GENERAL ADMINISTRATION

GARAGE ELEVATOR

GARAGE

LOBBY

SWIMMING POOL AND RECREATION AREA

FRONT DESK

GUEST ELEVATORS

RESTAURANTS AND BARS

GUEST ROOMS

LINEN CHUTE

GUEST ROOMS

SERVICE ELEVATORS

SOILED LINEN ROOM

OTHER AREAS

VALET SERVICE

BAGGAGE ROOM

LINEN SORTING

LAUNDRY

ACTIVE LINEN

PNEUMATIC TUBE TO FRONT DESK

PERSONNEL OFFICE

LOCKERS AND TOILETS

UNIFORM ROOM

HOUSEKEEPING OFFICE

CIRCULATION (SERVICE)

INACTIVE LINEN

LOST AND FOUND

SECURITY AND TIMEKEEPER'S OFFICE

TELEPHONE SWITCHBOARD

BACK OF THE HOUSE

EMPLOYEE'S ENTRANCE

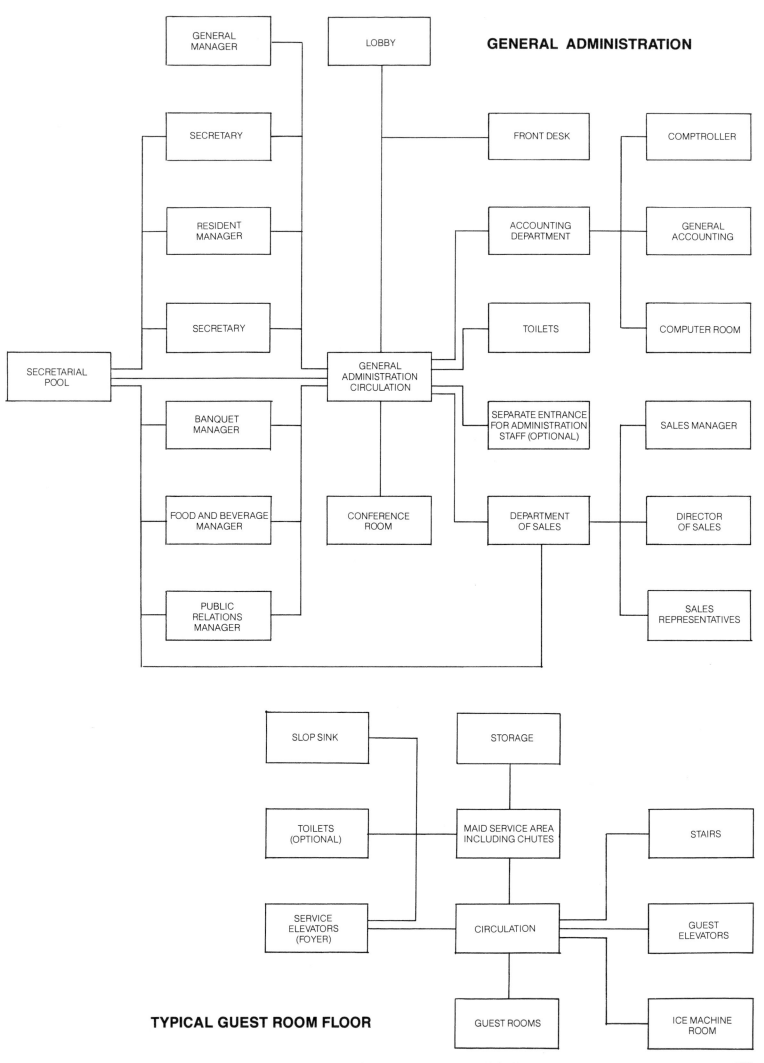

GENERAL ADMINISTRATION

GENERAL MANAGER

LOBBY

SECRETARY

RESIDENT MANAGER

SECRETARY

SECRETARIAL POOL

BANQUET MANAGER

FOOD AND BEVERAGE MANAGER

PUBLIC RELATIONS MANAGER

GENERAL ADMINISTRATION CIRCULATION

CONFERENCE ROOM

FRONT DESK

ACCOUNTING DEPARTMENT

TOILETS

SEPARATE ENTRANCE FOR ADMINISTRATION STAFF (OPTIONAL)

DEPARTMENT OF SALES

COMPTROLLER

GENERAL ACCOUNTING

COMPUTER ROOM

SALES MANAGER

DIRECTOR OF SALES

SALES REPRESENTATIVES

TYPICAL GUEST ROOM FLOOR

SLOP SINK

STORAGE

TOILETS (OPTIONAL)

MAID SERVICE AREA INCLUDING CHUTES

STAIRS

SERVICE ELEVATORS (FOYER)

CIRCULATION

GUEST ELEVATORS

GUEST ROOMS

ICE MACHINE ROOM

HYATT'S ARCHITECTURAL STANDARDS

FF&E BUDGET ITEMS	CONSTRUCTION BUDGET ITEMS
. ALL MOVEABLE FURNITURE	. LABOR FOR SECURING OF WALL-HUNG FURNITURE.
. ALL ART WORK INCLUDING PICTURES OR ANY OTHER TYPE OF ART WORK THAT WILL BE HUNG IN ALL ROOMS AND SUITES.	. HANGING OR PLACING ON WALLS OR CEILINGS OF ART WORK, MURALS AND OTHER DECORATIVE ITEMS.
. ALL CARPET AND CARPET PADDING AS WELL AS COST OF LAYING OF SAME.	. SPECIAL SCREEDS AND CEMENT FINISHES READY TO TAKE CARPETS.
. ALL DRAPERIES AND INSTALLATION THEREOF.	. SUPPLY AND INSTALLATION OF ALL HARDWARE NECESSARY TO HANG DRAPERIES (TO BE KIRSH HEAVY DUTY OF ADJUSTABLE TYPE AS PER HI STANDARDS).
. TELEVISION SETS.	. ELECTRICAL SUPPLY AS WELL AS, MASTER ANTENNA SYSTEM AS PER HYATT INTERNATIONAL ENGINEERING STANDARDS.
. ROOM STATUS SYSTEM.	. IN CASE THE ROOM STATUS SYSTEM IS NOT OF THE ELECTRONIC TYPE USING TELEPHONE WIRING FOR COMMUNICATION WITH THE TERMINALS, INSTALL SPECIAL CONDUITS AS REQUIRED.
. SUPPLY OF ROOM NUMBERING, DIRECTIONAL SIGNS, SIGNS FOR PUBLIC SPACES IDENTIFICATION.	. AFFIXING OR HANGING OF IDENTIFICATION AND DIRECTIONAL SIGNS AT LOCATIONS SHOWN ON ARCHITECTS DRAWINGS. SUPPLY AND INSTALLATION OF ELECTRIC SERVICE AND LIGHTING FIXTURES AS NECESSITATED BY ILLUMINATED SIGNS. SUPPLY AND INSTALLATION OF MAJOR BUILDING IDENTIFICATION SIGNS, (ROOF TOP, ENTRANCE CANOPY, ETC.).
	. ALL DECORATIVE CEILINGS AND WALL PANELINGS AS DESIGNED BY INTERIOR DESIGNERS.
	. ALL DOOR AND BATHROOM HARDWARE.

FF&E BUDGET ITEMS	CONSTRUCTION BUDGET ITEMS
. STANDARD MANUFACTURED ITEMS ("BUYOUTS") SUCH AS RANGES, FRYERS, OVENS, PEELERS, MIXERS, DISHWASHERS, GLASSWASHERS AND BURNISHING MACHINES. ALSO, SHELVING FOR FOOD AND BEVERAGE STORAGE AS WELL AS, FOR WALK-IN REFRIGERATORS.	. ALL PLUMBING, STEAM, ELECTRICAL AND VENTILATION CONNECTIONS FOR KITCHEN EQUIPMENT INCLUDING FINAL CONNECTION FROM THE ROUGHING IN POINT TO VARIOUS POINTS ON THE EQUIPMENT.
. FABRICATED EQUIPMENT ("PURPOSE BUILT OR CUSTOM BUILT") INCLUDING ITEMS SUCH AS COUNTERS, TABLES, POT AND DISHWASHING ARRANGEMENTS, ETC.	. ALL CUTTING AND PATCHING OF WALLS TO ACCOMMODATE EQUIPMENT.
. VENTILATION SYSTEMS AND/OR CANOPIES AND HOODS.	. SERVICES TO CANOPIES AND HOODS INCLUDING DUCT WORK, EXTRACTION SYSTEM OR FIRE DAMPENING. NECESSARY FLUES AND/OR VENTS OF SIZE AND CAPACITY REQUIRED TO OPERATE FIXTURES SPECIFIED TOGETHER WITH FINAL CONNECTION BETWEEN ROUGHED IN OPENINGS AND FIXTURES.
	. VENTILATING FANS AND ALL DUCT WORK, INCLUDING INSULATION WHEN REQUIRED, BETWEEN SAME AND FIXTURES AND FROM SAME TO DISCHARGE OPENING IN BUILDING.
	. DUCT WORK FOR KITCHEN EXTRACTION SHALL BE OF SPECIFIED GAUGE GALVANIZED STEEL WITH ALL WELDED CONSTRUCTION AND SHALL NOT BE COMBINED WITH GENERAL EXHAUST SYSTEM OR EXHAUST OF DISHWASH-ING, URNS, ETC. INSULATION OF MAIN KITCHEN EXHAUST SHALL BE OF THE FIRE RESISTANT TYPE OF MAGNESIUM BLOCK FINISHED WITH SMOOTH COST OF ASBESTOS PLASTER.
. ICE MAKING EQUIPMENT REQUIRED FOR FOOD AND BEVERAGE SERVICE AS WELL AS, UNITS LOCATED ON GUEST ROOM FLOORS.	. FOR REFRIGERATION WORK, ALL FINAL CONNECTIONS SUCH AS REFRIGERATION AND PLUMBING CONNECTIONS TO COMPRESSOR, BLOWER COILS, CONTROL ETC. IF NECESSARY, WATER COOLING TOWERS AS WELL AS, ALL WATER PIPING FROM COOLING TOWER

FF&E BUDGET ITEMS	CONSTRUCTION BUDGET ITEMS
. ALL STANDARD REACH-IN AND UNDER COUNTER REFRIGERATORS AND THEIR REFRIGERATION SYSTEMS.	AND/OR MAIN SOURCE TO WATER COOLED CONDENSERS AND RETURN LINE FOR SAME. ALL WIRING FROM PANELS TO CONDENSERS, EVAPORATORS, SAFETY CUTOUTS, ETC. FOR EACH OF THE SYSTEMS.
. WALK-IN REFRIGERATORS EITHER PREFABRICATED SECTIONAL TYPE OR BUILT-IN PLACE; AS SPECIFIED.	
. COMPLETE REFRIGERATION SYSTEMS, INCLUDING CONDENSING UNIT, EVAPORATORS AND PIPING.	
. SUPPLY MIXING VALVES FOR STEAM CLEANING OF KITCHEN, GARBAGE ROOM AND RECEIVING DOCK AREA.	. ALL TRAPS, GREASE TRAPS, TAIL PIECES, VALVES, STOPS, SHUT-OFFS, AND FITTINGS.
. WIRE ENCLOSURES OVER SERVICE BAR, STOREROOM, ETC.	. ALL LINE SWITCHES, SAFETY CUTOUTS, CONTROL PANELS, FUSE BOXES AND/OR OTHER ELECTRICAL CONTROLS, FITTINGS AND CONNECTIONS. ANY SLEEVES OR CONDUITS IN FLOOR SLAB OR WALLS, REQUIRED FOR REFRIGERATION, CARBONATED WATER OR CO$_2$ TUBING.
. THE KITCHEN EQUIPMENT CONTRACTOR IS ALSO RESPONSIBLE FOR:	
1 SETTING IN PLACE OF ALL EQUIPMENT.	. TILE OR CONCRETE BASES ARE TO BE FURNISHED AND INSTALLED IN COORDINATION WITH KITCHEN, PLUMBING AND ELECTRICAL CON-TRACTOR TO BE CERTAIN THAT OPENING OF SUFFICIENT SIZE WITHIN THE PERIMETER OF THE BASES ARE LEFT TO ACCOMMODATE ANY TRAP OR FITTING TO BE INSTALLED BELOW SHELVES OF FIXTURE.
2 COORDINATING AND ASSISTING THE MECHANICAL, ELECTRICAL AND PLUMB-ING SUBCONTRACTORS, WHO ARE RE-SPONSIBLE FOR MAKING THE ACTUAL UTILITY CONNECTIONS TO THE KITCHEN EQUIPMENT.	
3 TESTING OF ALL EQUIPMENT IN CON-JUNCTION WITH PLUMBING, ELECTRICAL AND AIR CONDITIONING SUBCONTRAC-TORS AND LOCAL AUTHORITIES IF RE-QUIRED BY LOCAL CODES.	. ALL DEPRESSIONS IN SLAB TO RECEIVE EQUIPMENT SUCH AS COUNTER SUNK SCALES, STEAM KETTLES, GRATES OVER DRAINAGE POINTS AND WALK-IN REFRIGERATORS.
4 ONE (1) YEAR FREE SERVICE ON ALL EQUIPMENT INCLUDING REFRIGERATION.	

FF&E BUDGET ITEMS	CONSTRUCTION BUDGET ITEMS
. ALL OPERATING EQUIPMENT SUCH AS:	. ERECTION OF MASONRY COUNTER.
ROOM RACKS	. ALL NECESSARY UTILITIES TO BE BROUGHT TO THESE MASONRY BASES.
CURRENT RESERVATION RACKS	
INFORMATION RACKS	. CONNECTION OF EQUIPMENT TO UTILITIES.
MAIL AND KEY RACKS	
TIME STAMPS	. ALL MILLWORK RELATED TO THE COUNTER AS PER HI AND INTERIOR DESIGNER SPECIFICATIONS.
POSTING MACHINES	
POSTING TRAYS	1 EXTERIOR FINISHES TO BE GIVEN BY INTERIOR DESIGNER.
ROOM MANAGEMENT SYSTEMS	
GUESTS SAFE DEPOSIT BOXES	2 INTERIOR LAYOUT TO BE PROVIDED BY HI TO ACCOMODATE THE OPERAT-ING EQUIPMENT.
CASHIER SAFES	
	. LABOR FOR INSTALLATION OF OPERATING EQUIPMENT.

FF&E BUDGET ITEMS	CONSTRUCTION BUDGET ITEMS
. SUPPLY AND INSTALLATION OF ALL KITCHEN EQUIPMENT AS PER KITCHEN CONSULTANT'S DRAWINGS AND SPECIFICATIONS.	. ALL MASONRY COUNTERS FOR BARS, SNACK BARS, DISPLAY KITCHENS, ETC AS WELL AS, MASONRY BINS UNDER ICE MACHINES.
	. FINISHING AND MILLWORK FOR COUNTERS, FRONT AND BACK BARS, STORAGE CABINETS, ETC. AS PER COORDINATED INTERIOR DESIGNER AND KITCHEN CONSULTANT CONSTRUCTION DOCUMENTS.

FF&E BUDGET ITEMS	CONSTRUCTION BUDGET ITEMS
. ALL LAUNDRY AND DRY CLEANING EQUIPMENT SUCH AS WASHERS, EXTRACTORS, FLATWORK IRONERS, DRY CLEANING UNIT, PRESSING MACHINERY, ETC. . ALL ANCILLARY ITEMS SUCH AS TABLES, TRUCK TUBS, CANVAS BASKETS. . THE LAUNDRY PLANS AND SPECIFICATIONS CALL FOR THE SUCCESSFUL LAUNDRY CONTRACTOR TO SUBMIT FINAL DIMENSIONED PLANS, MECHANICAL SERVICE REQUIREMENT DRAWINGS AND CATALOGS, LABOR AND SUPERVISORY PERSONNEL TO OVERSEE THE UNPACKING AND SETTING IN PLACE OF ALL EQUIPMENT AND TO COORDINATE THE WORK OF THE PLUMBING, MECHANICAL AND ELECTRICAL CONTRACTORS. . TESTING OF ALL LAUNDRY EQUIPMENT BY SUCCESSFUL CONTRACTOR, PLUS ONE YEAR'S FREE SERVICE ON ALL EQUIPMENT.	. ALL PLUMBING, STEAM, ELECTRICAL AND VENTILATION CONNECTIONS FOR LAUNDRY EQUIPMENT INCLUDING CONNECTION FROM ROUGHING-IN POINTS TO VARIOUS CONNECTIONS OF THE EQUIPMENT. . ALL STEAM TRAPS, VALVES, SHUT-OFFS AND NECESSARY FITTINGS. . ALL LINE SWITCHES, SAFETY CUTOUTS, CONTROL PANELS, FUSE BOXES AND/OR OTHER ELECTRICAL CONTROLS, FITTINGS AND CONNECTIONS. . NECESSARY FLUES AND/OR VENTS OF SIZE AND CAPACITY REQUIRED TO OPERATE FIXTURES SPECIFIED TOGETHER WITH FINAL CONNECTION BETWEEN ROUGHED-IN VENT OPENINGS AND FIXTURES. . VENTILATING FANS AND ALL DUCT WORK INCLUDING INSULATION WHEN REQUIRED BETWEEN SAME AND FIXTURES AND FROM SAME TO DISCHARGE OPENING IN BUILDING. . DEPRESSIONS IN SLAB AND/OR FOR GRATES OVER DRAINAGE POINTS. . ALL BASES TO RECEIVE EQUIPMENT AS PER DRAWING OR INSTRUCTIONS FROM LAUNDRY CONTRACTOR.

FF&E BUDGET ITEMS	CONSTRUCTION BUDGET ITEMS
. ALL DECORATIVE LIGHTING FIXTURES INCLUDING THE FOLLOWING: CHANDELIERS HANGING FIXTURES WALL BRACKETS FLOOR LAMPS TABLE LAMPS FIXTURES CONTAINED IN ITEMS OF FURNITURE	. ALL NECESSARY EQUIPMENT, WIRING, SWITCHES AND OUTLETS TO SUPPLY POWER TO THE FIXTURES INCLUDED IN HYATT'S FF & E BUDGET. . HANDLING AND INSTALLATION OF FIXTURES INCLUDED IN HYATT'S FF & E BUDGET WITH THE EXCEPTION OF TABLES AND FLOOR LAMPS. . PURCHASING, HANDLING AND INSTALLATION OF ALL OTHER LIGHTING INSTRUMENTS IN THE ENTIRE HOTEL IN ACCORDANCE WITH DRAWINGS, SPECIFICATIONS AND DETAILS. . ALL DIMMING DEVICES AND ASSOCIATED EQUIPMENT SUCH AS PATCH PANELS, CONTRACTORS, ETC. . COLOR FILTERS FOR RECESSED EQUIPMENT AS REQUIRED. . INITIAL SUPPLY OF ALL BULBS FOR ALL FIXTURES. THE FOLLOWING PAGES LIST THE TYPES OF FIXTURES THAT ARE REQUIRED:

FF&E BUDGET ITEMS	CONSTRUCTION BUDGET ITEMS
	GUEST FLOORS: 1 RECESSED OR SURFACE MOUNTED LIGHT FOR GUEST ROOMS, BATH, FOYER, CLOSET, BALCONY, SERVICE AREA, ELEVATOR SERVICE FOYER, LINEN ROOMS AND STAIRS. 2 NON DECORATIVE FIXTURES FOR CORRIDORS AND ELEVATOR FOYER. SERVICE AREAS: 1 RECESSED OR SURFACE MOUNTED FLUORESCENT FOR KITCHENS, PANTRIES, STORAGE SPACE, LOCKER ROOMS, PASSAGES, WORK AREAS. EXPLOSION PROOF FIXTURES FOR PAINT WORKSHOP AND KITCHEN. 2 LOW PRICED DECORATIVE FIXTURES FOR EMPLOYEES' CAFETERIA. SURFACE MOUNTED FIXTURES FOR SERVICE STAIRS. PUBLIC SPACE: 1 (INCLUDING ALL RESTAURANTS, LOBBIES AND FUNCTION ROOMS) RECESSED LIGHTS FOR GENERAL ILLUMINATION, ACCENTS, WALL LIGHTING AND STEP LIGHTS. 2 THEATRICAL SPOTLIGHTS IN BALLROOM AND RESTAURANTS WHICH WILL HAVE ENTERTAINMENT FACILITIES. 3 FOLLOW SPOTLIGHTS FOR BALLROOM AND NIGHTCLUBS. 4 LIGHTS FOR DECORATIVE POOLS AND FOUNTAINS. 5 WORKLIGHTS UNDER BAR COUNTERS AND INSIDE DISPLAY KITCHEN HOODS.

FF&E BUDGET ITEMS	CONSTRUCTION BUDGET ITEMS

	EXTERIOR AND SITE:
	
	1 FLOODLIGHTING OF FACADE AND OTHER FEATURES.
	
	2 PARKING LOT ILLUMINATION.
	
	3 SWIMMING POOL AND WADING POOL LIGHTING: 12 VOLT SYSTEM.
	
	4 FIXTURES FOR LIGHTING OF TREES AND PATHWAYS.
	
	5 GENERAL:
	
	  A. EMERGENCY FIXTURES AS REQUIRED BY CODE.
	  B. ILLUMINATED EXIT SIGNS.
	
	6 ALL NECESSARY EQUIPMENT AND WIRING TO SUPPLY POWER TO THE ITEMS LISTED.
	
	7 ALL DIMMING DEVICES AND ASSOCIATED EQUIPMENT SUCH AS PATCH PANELS, CONTACTORS, ETC.
	
	8 "PORTABLE" FIXTURES USED FOR DISPLAY PURPOSES, WHICH FORM PART OF THE OPERATING EQUIPMENT FOR THE HOTEL.
	
	9 COLOR FILTERS FOR RECESSED EQUIPMENT AS REQUIRED.
	
	10 INITIAL INSTALLATION OF ALL GARDEN LIGHTING EQUIPMENT ALTHOUGH THIS EQUIPMENT WILL BE A "PORTABLE" NATURE.
	
	11 INITIAL SUPPLY OF ALL BULBS FOR ALL FIXTURES.

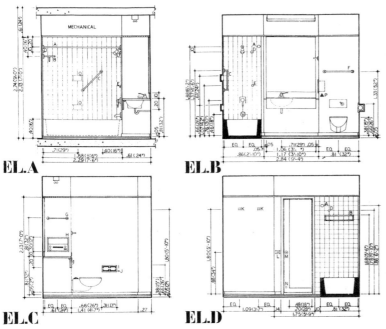

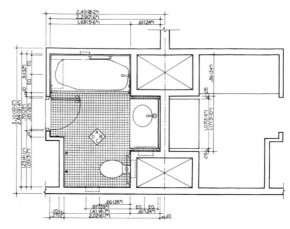

EL.A

EL.B

EL.C

EL.D

HARDWARE

STAINLESS STEEL, BRUSHED CHROME

A SHOWER ROD 1 1/4 DIAMETER
BOBRICK B204 OR EQUAL
B TOWEL SHELF AND BAR
BOBRICK B6767-24 OR EQUAL
C 45° GRAB BAR 1 1/4 DIAMETER
BOBRICK B 5507-24 OR EQUAL
D RETRACTABLE CLOTHES LINE
BOBRICK B436 OR EQUAL
E DOUCHE HOOK
F TOWEL BAR BOBRICK B6737-24
OR EQUAL
G TOWEL BAR BOBRICK B6737-18
OR EQUAL
H MULTIPURPOSE UNIT, KLEENEX,
BOTTLE OPENER, RAZOR BLADE
DISPOSAL, 2 CONVENIENCE OUTLETS

ACCEPTABLE TO AUTHORITIES
BOBRICK B3840 OR EQUAL

I DUAL TOILET PAPER HOLDER
BOBRICK B696 OR EQUAL
J SHOE CLOTH HOOK BOBRICK B222
OR EQUAL
K ROBE HOOK BOBRICK 6717 OR EQ.
L SWITCH PLATE SATIN FINISH
M DOOR KNOB PRIVACY TYPE SCHLAGE
D406 PLYMOUTH WITH SATIN STAIN-
LESS STEEL FINISH BATH SIDE
630(320)SATIN BRONZE ROOM SIDE
612(10)
N DOOR STOP SATIN FINISH
O SOAP DISHES RECESSED CERAMIC
TO MATCH TILES
P TELEPHONE EXTENSION OUTLET
SUITES ONLY

FINISHES

COORDINATE MATERIALS, COLORS, AND
PATTERNS W/INTERIOR DESIGNER.

FLOORS AND BASES MARBLE OR UNGLAZED
CERAMIC TILE.
TUB RECESS MARBLE OR GLAZED TILE
W/INTERIOR CURVED CORNERS.
WALLS VINYL WALL COVERING.
PLASTER CORNER BEADS ON ALL
VERTICAL CORNERS TO RECEIVE VINYL.
MIRRORS COPPER-BACKED MIRRORS,
ALLOW FOR EASY REPLACEMENT.
CEILING SUSPENDED METAL LATH AND
PLASTER OR FIXED PARTICLE BOARD OF
GOOD QUALITY, FINISH W/ENAMEL PAINT.

SANITARY FIXTURES

FIXTURES TO HAVE INDIVIDUAL SHUT-
OFF VALVES ACCESSIBLE FROM WITHIN
BATHROOM FOR EASY MAINTENANCE.

A BATHTUB ENAMELED CAST IRON W/FLAT
SLIP RESISTANT BOTTOM 66" MINIMUM
LENGTH. AMERICAN STANDARD
"CONTOUR" RECESSED TUB 2185.403
RIGHT OUTLET 2187.409 LEFT OUTLET
OR EQUAL.

AQUARIAN VALVE COLOR INDEXED
1390.160 OR EQUAL. SINGLE LEVER.
DIVERTER SPOUT 1623.065 OR EQ.
SHOWER ARM AND FLANGE 1444.017
OR EQUAL.
SHOWER HEAD 3 1/2" GPM OVERFLOW
1413.079 OR EQUAL.
POP UP DRAIN 1560.35 OR EQUAL.

B LAVATORY VITREOUS CHINA W/FRONT
OVERFLOW UNGLAZED RIM 19" X 16"
AMERICAN STANDARD OVALYN OR EQ.
AQUARIAN LAVATORY FAUCET CERAMIC
DISC CARTRIDGE, COLOR INDEXED,
ACRYLIC-CHROME LEVER HANDLE, 1/2"
MALE THREADED CONNECTOR INLETS, 4"
CENTERS, AERATOR, CHROME FINISH W/
POP UP DRAIN 2179.133 OR EQUAL.
SUPPLIES 3/8" W/LOOSE KEY STOPS
2303.063.
P TRAP W/17 GUAGE TUBING, CLEAN
OUT PLUG, ESCUTCHEON AND CHROME
FINISH 4401.014 OR EQUAL.

C WATER CLOSET VITREOUS CHINA
WALL MOUNTED RECESSED TANK TYPE
IDEAL STANDARD LARISSA BOWL
K338900 W/SEAT AND COVER AND
WALL CARRIER MK111A OR EQUAL.

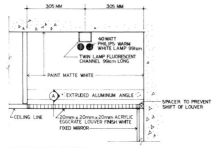

VANITY LIGHT SECTION

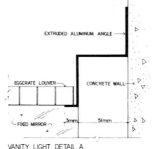

VANITY LIGHT DETAIL A

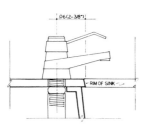

FAUCET DETAIL

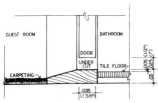

DOOR SILL DETAIL

LIGHTING

ALL LIGHT FIXTURES TO BE APPROVED
BY ELECTRICAL CONSULTANT.

LIGHT SWITCHES TO BE MERCURY TYPE
LOCATED OPPOSITE SIDE OF DOOR OPEN-
ING INSIDE BATHROOM IF ACCEPTABLE
TO LOCAL AUTHORITIES.

VANITY LIGHT TWIN LAMP FLUORESCENT
CHANNEL CEILING MOUNTED CENTERED
OVER VANITY 991 CM (39") LONG WITH
PHILIPS 40 WATT WARM WHITE LAMPS.
NOTE: USE A PRISMATIC ACRYLIC
DIFFUSER ABOVE COUNTERS OF SPECULAR
FINISHES, DO NOT USE OPEN LOUVERS.

BATHROOM ENCLOSURE

EXTEND ENCLOSING WALLS TO STRUCTURAL
SLAB ABOVE IN ALL CASES. INSURE THAT
ALL PENETRATIONS OF ENCLOSING WALLS
ABOVE OR BELOW SUSPENDED CEILING
ARE SLEEVED AND SECURELY CAULKED AND
THAT WALLS ARE AIR-TIGHT AND WITHOUT
CRACKS, TO INSURE PRESERVATION OF
THEIR ACCOUSTIC VALUE.

FLOORS · BASES · WALLS · CEILINGS

Area	Carpet	Unglazed Ceramic Tiles	Ceramic Tiles	Vinyl Asbestos Tiles	Concrete	Hard Surface	Quarry Tiles	Marble/Stone	Ceramic Tiles (base)	Vinyl Cove Base	Marble/Stone (base)	Pending Interior Design (base)	Vinyl Wall Covering	Plaster Paint (wall)	Cement Plaster	Ceramic Tiles (wall)	Painted Masonry	Paneling	Pending Interior Design (wall)	Plaster Paint (ceil)	Lath	Plaster on Metal	Acoustical Tiles	Acoustical Tiles	Aluminum Clad	Painted Concrete	Coffered Ceiling	Pending Interior Design (ceil)
GUEST FLOORS																												
Guest Room	●												●							●								
Foyer	●												●															●
Bathroom		●							●				●			●						●						
Corridors	●												●															●
Guest Elev. Lobbies	●																		●									●
Service Pantries			●							●						●				●								
Linen Rooms			●							●				●						●								
Service Elev. Lobbies			●							●				●						●								
Service and Fire Stairs					●												●									●		
RECEPTION																												
Front Desk Area			●							●									●									●
Cashiers			●							●									●									●
Front Desk Mgr.			●							●				●										●				
Credit Manager			●							●				●										●				
Secretary			●							●				●										●				
Reservations			●							●				●										●				
Guest Safes			●							●														●				
EXECUTIVE																												
Secretary and Waiting	●												●											●				
General Manager	●												●											●				
Conference Room	●												●											●				
Resident Manager	●												●											●				
Assistant Manager	●												●											●				
MEDICAL SUITE																												
Doctor's Office			●							●			●											●				
Examination Room			●							●			●											●				
Nurse and Waiting			●							●			●											●				
Storage			●							●				●						●								
Toilet		●							●							●				●								
BUSINESSMEN CENTER																												
Receptionist	●												●											●				
Office Cubicles	●												●											●				
Clerical Area	●												●											●				
Photocopying			●							●			●											●				
Telex and Telephone	●												●											●				
Storage			●							●				●						●								
SALES																												
Food and Beverage Manager			●							●				●										●				
Public Relations			●							●				●										●				
Banquet Manager			●							●				●										●				
Director of Sales	●									●				●										●				
Sales Office			●							●				●										●				
Secretaries			●							●				●										●				
AUDITING																												
Chief Auditor	●									●				●										●				
Auditing Office			●							●				●										●				
General Cashier			●							●				●										●				
Paymaster			●							●				●										●				

FLOORS · BASES · WALLS · CEILINGS

Room	CARPET	UNGLAZED CERAMIC TILES	TILES	VINYL ASBESTOS TILES	HARD SURFACE CONCRETE	QUARRY TILES	MARBLE / STONE	CERAMIC TILES	VINYL COVE BASE	MARBLE / STONE	PENDING INTERIOR DESIGN	VINYL WALL COVERING	PLASTER PAINT	CEMENT PLASTER	CERAMIC TILES	PAINTED MASONRY	PANELING	PENDING INTERIOR DESIGN	PLASTER PAINT	PLASTER ON METAL LATH	ACOUSTICAL TILES	ACOUSTICAL TILES	ALUMINUM CLAD	PAINTED CONCRETE	COFFERED CEILING	PENDING INTERIOR DESIGN
MAIN LOBBY																										
LOBBY AREA							●		●	●								●								●
PUBLIC TELEPHONES				●								●									●					
LUGGAGE STORAGE				●										●					●							
LAVATORIES		●						●							●					●						
SHOPS																										
BARBER SHOP				●								●									●					
BEAUTY PARLOR STYLING AND WASHING				●								●									●					
DRYING AND MANICURE	●											●									●					
TOILETS AND LABORATORY		●													●											
RENTAL AND CONCESSIONS	STORE FRONT, MASONRY ENCLOSURES, ACOUSTICAL TILES CEILING, AND UNFINISHED CONCRETE FLOOR TO BE PROVIDED IN CONSTRUCTION CONTRACT. SPECIAL FINISHES BY TENANTS.																									
DINING BARS																										
COFFEE SHOP	●										●							●								●
SPECIALTY RESTAURANT	●										●							●								●
BAR	●										●							●								●
COCKTAIL LOUNGE	●										●							●								●
NIGHTCLUB	●										●							●								●
ENTERTAINERS DRESSING ROOM				●					●			●									●					
CASINO	●										●							●								●
CROUPIERS LOUNGE	●											●										●				
STAFF CAFETERIA				●					●				●									●				
FUNCTION ROOMS																										
PRE FUNCTION	●										●						●	●								●
BALLROOM	●										●						●	●							●	●
PRIVATE DINING ROOMS	●										●							●								●
MEETING ROOMS	●										●							●								●
LAVATORIES		●						●							●							●				
PROJECTION ROOM				●					●					●					●							
BANQUET STORAGE					●											●								●		
RECREATIONAL FACILITIES																										
LOCKERS				●					●			●										●				
SHOWERS AND TOILETS		●						●							●								●			
WHIRLPOOL		●						●							●								●			
SAUNA AREA		●						●							●											
EXERCISE ROOM	●											●										●				
REST CUBICLES	●											●										●				
GAMES ROOM	●											●										●				
SWIMMING POOL AREA		●																								
EMPLOYEES ENTRANCE																										
TIMEKEEPER				●					●				●						●							
PERSONNEL DEPARTMENT				●					●				●						●							
PAYROLL				●					●				●						●							
STAFF LOCKERS				●					●				●						●							
STAFF TOILETS AND SHOWERS		●						●							●				●							
LAUNDRY																										
LAUNDRY ROOM				●											●				●							
WASHING AREA IN LAUNDRY ROOM				●											●				●							
VALET						●									●				●							
SOILED LINEN				●											●				●							
HOUSEKEEPING																										
HOUSEKEEPER AND ASSIST. OFF.				●				●				●								●						
STORAGE AND UNIFORM ROOM			●					●				●							●							
SEWING ROOM								●				●														
LOST AND FOUND				●												●								●		
HOUSEKEEPING SUPPLY ROOM				●													●							●		

190

Room finish schedule — groups: **FLOORS**, **BASES**, **WALLS**, **CEILINGS**

Room	CARPET	UNGLAZED CERAMIC TILES	VINYL TILES	VINYL ASBESTOS	HARD SURFACE CONCRETE	QUARRY TILES	MARBLE / STONE	CERAMIC TILES	VINYL COVE BASE	QUARRY TILES	PENDING INTERIOR DESIGN	VINYL WALL COVERING	PLASTER PAINT	CEMENT PLASTER	CERAMIC TILES	PAINTED MASONRY	PANELING	PENDING INTERIOR DESIGN	PLASTER PAINT	PLASTER ON METAL LATH	ACOUSTICAL TILES	ALUMINUM CLAD ACOUSTICAL TILES	PAINTED CONCRETE	PENDING INTERIOR DESIGN / COFFERED CEILING
KITCHENS																								
MAIN KITCHEN						●				●					●							●		
PANTRY						●				●					●							●		
DRY STORAGE					●											●							●	
LOADING AREA																								
RECEIVING AREA					●											●							●	
LOADING PLATFORM					●											●							●	
RECEIVING CLERK			●					●				●							●					
PURCHASING AGENT			●						●			●							●					
EMPTIES					●											●							●	
TRASH ROOM					●											●							●	
TEMPORARY FOOD STORAGE					●											●							●	
REFRIGERATORS, FREEZERS AND REFRIGERATED GARBAGE	MASONRY ENCLOSURES AND UNFINISHED CONCRETE FLOORS TO BE PROVIDED IN CONSTRUCTION CONTRACT. FOR EXACT TYPE AND CONSTRUCTION OF UNITS, REFER TO KITCHEN EQUIPMENT SPECIFICATIONS.																							
STORAGE																								
GENERAL STORAGE					●											●							●	
LUGGAGE STORAGE					●											●							●	
FURNITURE STORAGE					●											●							●	
GLASS CHINA AND SILVER STORAGE					●											●							●	
STATIONERY STORAGE					●											●							●	
WORKSHOPS																								
UPHOLSTERY					●											●							●	
PAINT					●											●							●	
CARPENTRY					●											●							●	
LOCKSMITH					●											●							●	
T.V. RADIO AND ELECTRICAL					●											●							●	
PLUMBING					●											●							●	
PRINTING					●											●							●	
ENGINEERING																								
CHIEF ENGINEER AND ASSIST. OFF.			●					●				●									●			
PLAN AND FILES ROOM			●					●				●									●			
ENGINEERING STORAGE					●											●							●	
ENG. LOCKERS & TOILETS		●						●							●					●				
MECHANICAL																								
TRANSFORMER					●											●							●	
BOILER ROOM					●											●							●	
AIR CONDITIONING					●											●							●	
FAN ROOM					●											●							●	
ELEC. EQUIP. ROOM			●									●							●					
ELECTRIC SWITCHBOARD			●						●			●							●					
TELEPHONE EQUIPMENT			●						●			●							●					
TELEPHONE OPERATORS			●						●			●									●			

191

DEFINITION OF SCOPE OF TYPICAL FURNISHING AND/OR EQUIPMENT BUDGET USED BY HENRY END ASSOCIATES

Henry End Associates furnishing and equipment budgets are complete with regard to equipment, furniture, and furnishings. Very often, however, a question arises as to what items are covered in this budget. The purpose of the following pages is to define as clearly as possible which items are contained in the Henry End Associates' budget so that remaining items can be covered in construction, mechanical, or other budgets or work.

This is not a set of specifications, but a guideline to be used in the establishment of specifications, and it is particularly important that the architects specify and provide in their budget and specifications for items not covered.

We are merely attempting to establish a demarcation line between the so-called Henry End Associates budget and the construction budget as well as indicating the minimum standard of finishes to be provided by the general contractor that will be acceptable to Henry End Associates. The finishes for all areas will still have to be finally approved by Henry End Associates and the cost of detailing of plans and specifications and the following details are meant to give guidance to owners, general contractors, subcontractors, etc., for their initial estimation of general construction costs.

1. **Furniture, furnishings, and interior decoration**

A. Guest room suites and corridors

1. The Henry End Associates budget in the amount of . . . includes the following:

a. All movable furniture.

b. All art work, including pictures, tapestries, or any other type of art work that will be hung in all rooms and suites.

c. All carpeting and carpet padding as well as cost of laying of same.

d. All draperies and curtains, hooks and rings, and installation of draperies and curtain hardware.

e. All decorative lighting fixtures such as brackets, floor lamps, and table lamps.

2. This budget, however, does not cover the following items and provision must be made for them in the general contract or in other subcontracts:

a. Labor for securing of wall-hung furniture.

b. Hanging or placing on walls or ceilings of art work, murals, and other decorative items.

c. Special screeds and cement finishes ready to take carpets.

d. Hardware for curtains.

3. Suggested finishes: to be provided for in the general contract. Adequate budgetary allocations must be considered for these finishes, bearing in mind that they are the minimum acceptable to Henry End Associates.

a. Rooms

1. Floors: screed ready to take wall to wall carpeting.

2. Walls: at least one wall to be covered with washable wall covering. Balance will be accepted in painted plaster provided plastering is of excellent quality.

3. Ceiling: painted plaster.

4. Closet: minimum size to be 6 ft (1.8 m) in width and 2 ft (.6 m) in depth. Unless otherwise specified, doors should be of the bifolding type. Hardware, shelving, as well as lighting to be included in general contract.

Whenever possible, access for shoe cleaning to be incorporated in bottom of closet.

5.   Electrical: electrical contractor to supply recessed or other type of lights and switches as per outline specifications that are issued by Henry End Associates.

b. Bathroom

1.   Floor: ceramic, glass, or mosaic tiles (color and type to be approved by Henry End Associates).

2.   Ceiling: painted plaster, sprayed or hung-acoustical ceiling depending on special conditions.

3.   Wash basin counter: marble or plastic laminate with builtin bowl.

4.   Lighting: as lighting in bathroom is especially important, a sketch is attached with full details that will naturally have to be adapted to the specific conditions of the bathroom.

5.   Hardware: this is fully detailed in the outline specs issued by Henry End Associates.

c. Corridor

1.   Floor: screed ready to receive wall-to-wall carpeting.

2.   Walls: plastic wall covering, grasscloth, or vinyl.

3.   Ceiling: acoustical ceiling with possibility of recessed lighting. Adequate electrical wiring to be available for the possibility of incorporating wall-mounted decorative lighting.

d. Elevator landings

1.   Floors: marble or carpet.

2.   Walls: plastic wall covering, grass cloth, or vinyl.

3.   Ceiling: acoustically treated.

e. Service elevator landings

1. Floor: vinyl tile.

2. Walls: painted plaster.

3. Ceiling: acoustical tiles.

4. Closets: all shelving to be included in general contract according to design supplied by Henry End Associates.

5. Chutes: both trash and linen chutes to be located in this area. Must have minimum specs.

6. Slop sink: to be incorporated in this general area. Please refer to plumbing specs.

7. Doors to landing: will have kick plate protection on both sides as well as closers that will have a time device

B.   Public areas

1.   The Henry End Associates budget in the amount of . . . includes the following:

a. All movable furniture.

b. All art work, including pictures, panels, and tapestries.

c. All carpeting and carpet padding as well as laying of same.

d. All draperies and curtains, hooks and rings, and installation of curtains and drapes on hardware.

e. All decorative lighting such as wall brackets, chandeliers, floor lamps, table lamps.

2.   This budget does not cover the following items and provisions must be made for this in the general contract or other subcontracts:

a. Labor for securing of wall-hung furniture.

b. Hanging or placing on walls or ceiling all art works, murals, and other decorative items such as heavy chandeliers, decorative panels.

c. Special screeds and cement finishes ready to take carpet. When carpets are not specifically indicated, general contractor should include special floor finishes as indicated below.

d. Builtin hardware and curtain rods placed in walls and ceiling for draperies and curtains as well as labor for their installation.

e. All recessed down lights and their installation including dimmers and other such controls.

f. Erection of all masonry counters that will serve as base for bar counters, coffee shop counters, front office counters as well as the finishes on these counters. All necessary utilities to be brought to these masonry bases by electrical and plumbing contractor as well as connections to utilities of equipment will have to be foreseen by the general contractor.

3. Suggested finishes: to be provided for in the general contract. Adequate budget allocation must be considered for these finishes bearing in mind that they are the minimum acceptable to Henry End Associates.

a. Lobby and lounges

1. Floors: marble, tile, or terrazzo.

2. Walls: marble, wood paneling, special textured painted plaster.

3. Ceiling: must be specially designed. At this point, exact finish cannot be determined but adequate budget allocation must be made for a specially hung ceiling with all adequate builtin lights. Whatever the shape of the ceiling, it must include acoustical plaster or covering to absorb noises.

b. Main and other restaurants

1. Floor: screed ready to receive wall-to-wall carpeting.

2. Walls: wood paneling or other such finishes.

3. Ceiling: here again, the ceiling will have to be specially designed but it will have to include acoustical ceiling with builtin lighting. Adequate provision must be made for specialty items such as beams.

c. Coffee shop

1. Floor: vinyl tile or carpet.

2. Walls: painted plaster or wall covering.

3. Ceiling: acoustical material with builtin lighting.

4. Counter: erection as well as finish on top and front must be included in general contract. Foot railing as well as finish on side could be wood, marble, glass, mosaic, or vinyl. Top counter could be plastic laminate or wood.

d. Bar

1. Floor: screed ready to take wall-to-wall carpeting.

2. Walls: wood paneling or other such finish.

3. Ceiling: textured material with decorative features. Must be acoustical material.

4. Bar counter: front to be covered in wood or other such material. Top: wood or plastic laminate.

e. Ballroom

1. Floor: parquet, carpet, or combination of both.

2. Walls: covered by material vinyl; in certain areas with mirrors.

3. Ceiling: decorative ceiling, three dimensional or vaulted. Acoustical material to be used. Special theater lighting to be incorporated into ceiling.

f. Administrative areas

1. Floor: screed ready to take wall-to-wall carpeting.

2. Walls: painted plaster or wall covering.

3. Ceiling: acoustical material.

C. Decorative lighting

1. Henry End Associates budget in the amount of . . . includes the following:

a. Chandeliers.

b. Hanging fixtures.

c. Wall brackets.

d. Floor lamps.

e. Table lamps.

f. Fixtures contained in items of furniture.

2. This budget does not cover the following items and provision must be made for this in the general contract or other subcontracts.

a. All necessary equipment and wiring to supply power to the ornamental fixtures listed above.

b. Handling and installation of the ornamental fixtures listed above, except table and floor lamps.

c. Purchasing, handling, and installation of all other lighting instruments in the entire hotel in accordance with drawings, specifications, and details. The following or equivalent may be required:

(1) Guest floors

(a) Recessed or surface mounted light for guest rooms, bath, foyer, closet, balcony, service foyer, closets, and stairs.

(b) Wall brackets and/or other fixtures for corridors and elevator foyer.

(2) Service areas

(a) Recessed or surface mounted fluorescent or incandescent for kitchens, pantries, storage space, locker rooms, passages, work areas. Explosion-proof fixtures for paint workshop.

(b) Low-priced decorative fixtures for employees' cafeteria. Surface-mounted incandescent fixtures for service stairs.

(3) Public space

(a) (Including all restaurants, lobbies, and function rooms) recessed lights for general illumination, accents, wall lighting, and step lights.

(b) Theatrical spotlights (coupled to dimming board or console) in ballroom and restaurants which will have entertainment facilities.

(c) Follow spotlights for ballroom and night clubs.

(d) Lights for decorative pools and fountains.

(e) Worklights under bar counters and inside rotisserie hoods.

(4) Exterior and site

(a) Floodlighting of facade and other features.

(b) Parking lot illumination.

(c) Swimming pool and wading pool lighting; low voltage system.

(d) Fixtures for lighting of trees and pathways.

(e) General: (1) Emergency fixtures as required by code. (2) Illuminated exit signs.

d. All necessary equipment and wiring to supply power to the items listed.

e. All dimming devices and associated equipment such as patch panels, contractors, etc.

f. "Portable" fixtures used for display purposes, which form part of the operating equipment for the hotel.

g. Color filters for recessed equipment as required.

h. Initial installation of all garden lighting equipment although this equipment will be of a "portable" nature.

i. Initial supply of all lighting bulbs for all fixtures.

2. Major equipment

A. Kitchen bar and refrigeration

1. Henry End Associates budget in the amount of . . . includes the following:

a. Cooking equipment such as ranges, fryers, ovens, etc.

b. Kitchen machines such as peelers, mixers.

c. Ware washing equipment such as dishwashers, glasswashers, burnishing machines.

d. Fabricated items such as table tops, sinks, bars, work area cabinets, drawers, shelves, etc.

e. Ventilation canopies and hoods (not including ductwork, extraction system, or fire damping equipment, steam smothering, or CO_2 fire-smothering system).

f. Ice-making equipment.

g. All reach-in and undercounter refrigerators and refrigeration systems.

h. In the case of large builtin, walkin refrigerators, the Henry End Associates specification covers only the complete refrigeration systems, including condensing unit, evaporators and piping, refrigerator shelving, thermometers, doors and hardware, but the construction, insulation, and finishing of these boxes, including the setting of the doors, should be provided for in the work of the general contractor. Alarm systems for the walkin refrigerators shall be provided by the general contractor.

i. Miscellaneous items such as receiving scale, garbage can washing unit, etc.

2. The Henry End Associates specification will call for a kitchen contractor to accept only the following responsibility in terms of work to be performed once a contract has been awarded:

a. Submission of mechanical layout, base drawings, detail drawing, including all service requirements, and catalog data on all standard manufactured items.

b. The taking of field dimensions necessary for fabrication of custom-built equipment and the coordination of standard manufactured items. Site visits will be included as required.

c. Setting in place of all equipment.

d. Coordinating and assisting the mechanical, electrical, and plumbing subcontractors, who are responsible for making the actual utility connections to the kitchen equipment.

e. Testing of all kitchen equipment.

f. One year free service on all equipment including refrigeration.

3. The following work is not a part of the work of the kitchen equipment contractor as defined under the Henry End Associates specifications for kitchen and bar equipment:

a. All plumbing, steam, electrical, and ventilation connections for kitchen equipment will be done by others. The work to be done by these other contractors shall include roughing-in to points indicated on mechanical plan and final connecting from the roughing-in point to various pieces of equipment requiring such connections as hereinafter noted.

For refrigeration work, all final connections will be made by other contractors as well as electrical and plumbing connections to compressor, blowing coils, control, etc. Water cooling towers, if necessary, will be supplied and installed by others as well as all cooling water piping from cooling tower and/or main source to water-cooled condensers and return line for same. This applies also to all wiring from panels to condensers, evaporators, safety cutouts, etc., for each of the systems.

b. All traps, grease traps, tail pieces, values, stops, shutoffs, and fittings necessary will be furnished and installed under mechanical contract by others. All exposed final plumbing connections to be chrome-plated.

c. All steam traps, valves, shut-offs, and fittings necessary shall be furnished and installed under mechanical contracts by others. Steam lines with mixing valves for steam cleaning of kitchen, garbage room, receiving dock area will be supplied and installed by others.

d. All line switches, safety cutouts, control panels, fuse boxes, and/or other electrical controls, fittings, and connections shall be furnished and installed by others.

e. All sleeves required for refrigeration, carbonated water, or CO_2 tubing will be furnished and installed under mechanical contract by others.

f. Necessary flues and/or vents of size and capacity required to operate fixtures specified together with final connection between rough-in vent openings and fixtures shall be furnished by other contractors.

g. Ventilating fans and all duct work, including insulation when required, between same and fixtures and from same to discharge opening in building shall be furnished and installed by others.

Duct work for kitchen extraction shall be of 10 gauge black steel with all-welded construction and shall not be combined with general exhaust system or exhaust of dishwashing, urns, etc. Insulating of main kitchen exhaust shall be of the fire-resistant type of magnesium block furnished with smooth coat of asbestos plaster.

h. Tile or concrete bases are to be furnished and installed by others in coordination with kitchen, plumbing, and electrical contractor to be certain that opening of sufficient size within the perimeter of the bases are left to accommodate any trap or fitting to be installed below shelves of fixture. It is mandatory that floors in all kitchen areas be supplied with nonskid quarry tiles. Walls will be covered with white, pale blue, or pale grey vitreous style. All corners on columns and walls will be protected with stainless steel angles. Ceilings will be of the suspended, washable, metallic type with special fireproof insulation.

i. Walkin refrigerators shall be constructed as shown on plan including tile, and/or plaster, insulation, vapor seal, door bucks, plumbing drain, etc.

When specifications call for splash backs or tops of fixtures to be extended into grooves cut into walls, the grouting of these grooves after the fixtures are set in place will be done by tile or plaster contractor. All depression in slab to receive equipment such as counter-suck scales, steam kettles, etc., will be done by others. All masonry counters for bars, snack bars, etc., as well as masonry bins under ice machines will be done by others. Wall tiles, floor quarry tiles, hung ceiling as well as corner angle protectors will be supplied and installed by others. All cutting and patching on walls to accommodate equipment will be done by others.

j. Wire enclosures over service bar, storeroom, etc., will be supplied and installed by others.

k. Grates over drainage points or over trough will be supplied and installed by others.

l. Miscellaneous items such as decorative counter, counter. tops, front and back bars, storage cabinet, etc., will be supplied and installed by others.

m. Air conditioning of finishing area in pastry shop and butcher shop and wine rooms is mandatory and shall be provided by others.

B. Laundry and dry cleaning

1. Henry End Associates budget in the amount of . . . includes the following:

a. All laundry and dry cleaning equipment such as washers, extractors, flatwork ironers, dry cleaning unit, pressing machinery, etc.

b. All ancillary items such as tables, truck tubs, canvas baskets.

c. The laundry plans and specifications call for the successful laundry contractor to submit final dimensioned plans, mechanical service requirement drawings and catalogs, labor and supervisory personnel to oversee the unpacking and setting in place of all equipment and to coordinate the work of the plumbing, mechanical, and electrical contractors, who are responsible for making the actual utility connections to the laundry equipment. Finally, to provide for the testing of all laundry equipment by successful contractor, plus one year's free service on all equipment.

2. This budget does not cover the following items and provision must be made for this in the general contract or other subcontracts.

a. All plumbing, steam, electrical, and ventilation connections for laundry equipment will be done by others. The work to be done by these other contractors shall include roughing-in points to various pieces of equipment requiring such connections as hereinafter noted.

b. All steam traps, valves, shut-offs, and necessary fittings shall be furnished and installed under mechanical contracts by others.

c. All line switches, safety cutouts, control panels, fuse boxes, and/or other electrical controls, fittings, and connections shall be furnished and installed by others.

d. Necessary flues and/or vents of size and capacity required to operate fixtures specified together with final connection between roughed-in vent openings and fixtures shall be furnished by others.

e. Ventilating fans and all ductwork including insulation when required between same and fixtures and from same to discharge opening in building shall be furnished and installed by others.

f. Grates over drainage points or over trough will be supplied and installed by others.

g. All bases to receive equipment will be made by others as per drawing or instructions from the laundry contractor.

HYATT'S TYPICAL FINISHING SCHEDULE

Area	Floor	Baseboard	Walls	Ceiling
Administration area				
Reception				
Front office	Vinyl tiles	Vinyl	Plaster/paint/ vinyl	Acoustic tiles/ plaster
Reservations	Vinyl tiles	Vinyl	Plaster/paint/ vinyl	Acoustic tiles/ plaster
General manager	Concrete lining/ carpet	Vinyl	Plaster/paint/ vinyl	Acoustic tiles/ plaster
Manager	Vinyl tiles	Vinyl	Plaster/paint/ vinyl	Acoustic tiles/ plaster
Assistant manager	Vinyl tiles	Vinyl	Plaster/paint/ vinyl	Acoustic tiles/ plaster
Secretaries	Vinyl tiles	Vinyl	Plaster/paint/ vinyl	Acoustic tiles/ plaster
Conference room	Concrete lining/ carpet	Vinyl	Plaster/paint/ vinyl	Acoustic tiles/ plaster
Sales department				
Credit manager	Vinyl tiles	Vinyl	Plaster/paint/ vinyl	Acoustic tiles/ plaster
Food and beverage manager	Vinyl tiles	Vinyl	Plaster/paint/ vinyl	Acoustic tiles/ plaster
Banquet manager	Concrete lining/ carpet	Vinyl	Plaster/paint/ vinyl	Acoustic tiles/ plaster
Public relations	Concrete lining/ carpet	Vinyl	Plaster/paint/ vinyl	Acoustic tiles/ plaster
Resident manager	Concrete lining/ carpet	Vinyl	Plaster/paint/ vinyl	Acoustic tiles/ plaster
Auditing department				
Chief auditor	Vinyl tiles	Vinyl	Plaster/paint/ vinyl	Acoustic tiles/ plaster
General cashier	Vinyl tiles	Vinyl	Plaster/paint/ vinyl	Acoustic tiles/ plaster
Paymaster	Vinyl tiles	Vinyl	Plaster/paint/ vinyl	Acoustic tiles/ plaster
Doctor's suite				
Waiting room	Vinyl tiles	Vinyl	Plaster/paint/ vinyl	Acoustic tiles/ plaster
Doctor's room	Concrete lining/ carpet	Vinyl	Plaster/paint/ vinyl	Acoustic tiles/ plaster
Shops				
Barber shop	Vinyl tiles	Vinyl	Plaster/paint/ vinyl	Acoustic tiles/ plaster
Beauty shop	Vinyl tiles	Vinyl	Plaster/paint/ vinyl	Acoustic tiles/ plaster
Flower shop	Vinyl tiles	Vinyl	Plaster/paint/ vinyl	Acoustic tiles/ plaster
Cigar stand	Vinyl tiles	Vinyl	Plaster/paint/ vinyl	Acoustic tiles/ plaster
Transportation	Vinyl tiles	Vinyl	Plaster/paint/ vinyl	Acoustic tiles/ plaster
Post office	Vinyl tiles	Vinyl	Plaster/paint/ vinyl	Acoustic tiles/ plaster

Boutiques	Vinyl tiles	Vinyl	Plaster/paint/vinyl	Acoustic tiles/plaster
Bank	Vinyl tiles	Vinyl	Plaster/paint/vinyl	Acoustic tiles/plaster
Dining area & bars				
Coffee shop	Concrete lining/carpet	Vinyl	Pending decor	Acoustic tiles/plaster
Dining room	Concrete lining/carpet	Marble/wood	Pending decor	Acoustic tiles/plaster
Grill room	Concrete lining/carpet	Marble/wood	Pending decor	Acoustic tiles/plaster
Bar	Concrete lining/carpet	Marble/wood	Pending decor	Acoustic tiles/plaster
Cocktail lounge	Concrete lining/carpet	Marble/wood	Pending decor	Acoustic tiles/plaster
Nightclub	Concrete lining/carpet/parquet dancing floor	Marble/wood	Pending decor	Acoustic tiles/plaster
Employees cafeteria	Vinyl tiles	Vinyl	Plaster/paint/vinyl	Acoustic tiles/plaster
Supervisors' dining room	Vinyl tiles	Vinyl	Plaster/paint/vinyl	Acoustic tiles/plaster
Function rooms				
Ballroom	Concrete lining/carpet/parquet	Marble/wood	Pending decor	Pending decor
Private dining rooms	Concrete lining/carpet	Marble/wood	Pending decor	Pending decor
Convention halls	Concrete lining/carpet	Marble/wood	Acoustic tiles/plaster	Acoustic tiles
Lobbies	Pending decor	Marble/wood	Pending decor	Pending decor
Corridors	Marble, terrazzo, or carpet	Marble or terrazzo	Plaster/paint/vinyl	Plaster/paint/vinyl
Lavatories	Ceramic tiles	Ceramic tiles	Ceramic tiles	Plaster/paint/vinyl
Kitchen				
Main kitchen	Quarry tiles	Ceramic tiles	Ceramic tiles	Metallic acoustic tiles
Food storage	Hard concrete	Ceramic tiles	Ceramic tiles	Metallic acoustic tiles
Freezers	Ceramic tiles	Ceramic tiles	Ceramic tiles	Plaster/tiles insulation
Beverage department	Hard concrete	Ceramic	Ceramic tiles	Plaster
Loading area				
Receiving area	Hard concrete		Finished cement plaster	Plaster
Loading platform	Hard concrete	Concrete tiles	Finished cement plaster	Plaster
Receiving clerk	Vinyl tiles	Vinyl	Plaster/paint	Acoustic tiles
Purchasing agent	Vinyl tiles	Vinyl	Plaster/paint	Acoustic tiles
Bottle room	Hard concrete	Concrete	Finished cement plaster	Plaster
Freight elevator	Metallic	Metallic	Metallic	Metallic
Temporary food storage	Hard concrete	Concrete tiles	Finished cement plaster	Plaster

Employees entrance

Timekeeper	Vinyl tiles	Vinyl	Plaster/paint	Acoustic tiles
Men's lockers	Ceramic tiles	Ceramic tiles	Ceramic tiles	Plaster/paint
Women's lockers	Ceramic tiles	Ceramic tiles	Ceramic tiles	Plaster/paint
Personnel department	Vinyl tiles	Vinyl	Plaster/paint	Acoustic tiles
Payroll	Vinyl tiles	Vinyl	Plaster/paint	Acoustic tiles

Laundry

Laundry room	Hard concrete	Ceramic tiles	Ceramic tiles	Plaster
Valet service	Hard concrete	Ceramic tiles	Ceramic tiles	Plaster
Soiled linen	Hard concrete	Ceramic tiles	Ceramic tiles	Plaster

Housekeeping

Housekeeper's office	Vinyl tiles	Vinyl	Plaster/paint	Plaster
Assistant housekeeper's office	Vinyl tiles	Vinyl	Plaster/paint	Plaster
Storage	Hard concrete	Concrete tiles	Plaster	Plaster
Uniform room	Hard concrete	Concrete tiles	Plaster	Plaster
Sewing room	Hard concrete	Concrete tiles	Plaster	Plaster
Lost and found room	Hard concrete	Concrete tiles	Plaster	Plaster
Housekeeper's supply room	Hard concrete	Concrete tiles	Plaster	Plaster

Storage

General storage	Hard concrete	Concrete tiles	Cement plaster	Cement plaster
Luggage room	Hard concrete	Concrete tiles	Terrazzo	Plaster
Furniture storage	Hard concrete	Concrete tiles	Plaster	Plaster
Glass, china, silver storage	Hard concrete	Concrete tiles	Plaster	Plaster
Stationery storage	Hard concrete	Concrete tiles	Plaster	Plaster

Workshops

Upholstery	Hard concrete	Concrete tiles	Cement plaster	Plaster
Paint	Hard concrete	Concrete tiles	Cement plaster	
Carpentry	Hard concrete	Concrete tiles	Cement plaster	
Locksmith	Hard concrete	Concrete tiles	Cement plaster	
TV/radio repair	Hard concrete	Concrete tiles	Cement plaster	Plaster
Mechanical	Concrete tiles	Concrete tiles	Terrazzo	Plaster

Engineering

Engineer, assistant offices	Vinyl tiles	Vinyl	Plaster/paint	Plaster
Engineering storage room	Hard concrete	Concrete tiles	Cement plaster	Plaster
Engineers' lockers	Ceramic tiles	Ceramic tiles	Ceramic tiles	Plaster/paint
Plan room	Vinyl tiles	Vinyl	Plaster/paint	Plaster/paint

Mechanical

Transformer	Hard concrete	Concrete tiles	Cement plaster	
Boiler room	Hard concrete	Concrete tiles	Cement plaster	
Air conditioning room	Hard concrete	Concrete tiles	Cement plaster	
Electric switchboard	Hard concrete	Concrete tiles	Plaster	Plaster
Machine room	Hard concrete	Concrete tiles	Cement plaster	
Fan room	Hard concrete	Concrete tiles	Cement plaster	Plaster
Electric equipment room	Vinyl tiles	Vinyl	Plaster/paint	Plaster
Telephone room	Vinyl tiles	Vinyl	Plaster/paint	Acoustic tiles
Telephone equipment room	Vinyl tiles	Vinyl	Plaster/paint	Plaster/paint

Incinerator

Incinerator room	Hard concrete		Cement plaster	
Garbage room	Hard concrete		Cement plaster	
Wastepaper room	Hard concrete		Cement plaster	

Food & beverage storage

Partial kitchen	Hard concrete	Concrete tiles	Cement plaster	Plaster

Typical floor

Guest room	Concrete lining/ carpet	Marble/wood	Plaster/paint	Plaster/paint
Bathroom	Ceramic tiles	Ceramic tiles	Ceramic tiles	Plaster/paint
Corridors	Concrete lining/ carpet	Marble/wood/ vinyl	Plaster/paint	Plaster/paint
Service	Ceramic tiles	Ceramic tiles	Ceramic tiles	Plaster/paint

Approximate Costs for Guest Room Furnishings in Howard Johnson Motor Lodges (1977) "A" Room*

Quantity	Furnishings	Price
1	Desk chair	$32.70
1	"A" room headboard, wall-hung	136.00
2	Lounge chairs, Naugahyde Grade 1 (each), @ $52.70 Soft-grade 3 (each), @ $63.35	126.70
1	"A" room triplex 4 drawers (std.), wall hung	252.00
	"A" room triplex 3 drawers @ $232.40, wall hung	
	"A" room triplex 2 drawers @ $212.80, wall hung	
1	"A" room coffee table	43.60
2 sets	Foam mattress and innerspring box units @ $123.45	246.90
1 pair	Draperies (installed) per room	120.00
1	Room and corridor carpet, including lining & installation, 37 sq yd	322.40
2	Bedframe, @ $13.85 each	27.70
2	Pictures, @ $16.95 each	33.90
2	Baskets, room	2.82
	bath	.89
Total		$1,345.61

Approximate Costs for Guest Room Furnishings in Howard Johnson Motor Lodges (1977) "D2" Room*

Quantity	Furnishings	Price
1	Desk chair	$32.70
1	"D2" room headboard, wall hung	89.05
2	Lounge chairs, Naugahyde Grade 1 (each), @ $52.70 Soft-grade 3 (each), @ $63.35	63.35
1	"D2" room triplex, wall hung	201.50
1	"D2" room coffee table each	40.35
1 set	Innerspring box unit foam mattress unit	123.45
1 pair	Draperies (installed) per room	120.00
1	Room and corridor carpet, including lining & installation 25 sq yd	233.00
1	Bedframe	13.85
2	Pictures, @ $16.95 each	33.90
2	Baskets, room	2.82
	bath	.89
Total		$954.86

*Prices FOB factory, mill, or shipping point. Allow additional 7–10 percent for freight. Plus 3–7 percent for sales tax. Prices are based on a minimum of 100 rooms and are approximate and subject to change without notice.

ASID CONTRACTS

American Society of Interior Designers

ASID Document 401

Contract for
**Professional Services:
Stipulated Sum**

This **CONTRACT** is

made this   day of   in the year of Nineteen
Hundred and

BETWEEN the Client:
(name & address)

and the Designer:
(name & address)

for the following Project:

Architectural firms which have rendered practically "free" interior design services to their clients will soon have a document enabling them to put these services on a paying basis. The American Institute of Architects and the American Society of Interior Designers (ASID) are entering the last stages of producing a contract which both architects and interior designers may use. The contract recommendation must be approved by both organizations. Copies are expected to be available in the fall of 1978.

1. PROFESSIONAL SERVICES

1.1 General: The Designer's professional services shall consist generally of consulting with the Client to determine scope of work; preparing the necessary preliminary studies; making preliminary estimates; preparing working drawings and specifications; advising in the drafting of forms of proposals, tenders and contracts and on proposals and tenders made; instructing or engaging architects, engineers or other special consultants, if required, and incorporating plans and specifications developed by any such special consultants into working drawings and specifications; furnishing to the contractor(s) such copies of the contract drawings and specifications, and detailed drawings to the extent indicated, as are appropriate for the carrying out of the Project; checking of shop drawings when considered appropriate by the Designer; the general observation of the Project; and preparing certificates for payments.

1.2 Preliminary Cost Estimates: The Designer will furnish to or obtain for the Client preliminary estimates of the cost of the Project. If requested the Designer will review, and if required revise, such estimates from time to time as the preparation of drawings and specifications proceeds. Definitive costs can only be expected when contract bids are received.

1.3 Observation of the Work: The Designer will perform or procure such periodic inspections as the Designer may consider appropriate, but constant observation of work on the Project does not form part of the Designer's duties. The Designer will endeavour to warn the Client against defects and deficiencies in the work of the contractor(s), but shall not have responsibility for the failure of a contractor(s) to comply with drawings or specifications or for any latent defect in such contractor(s) work.

1.4 Certificates for Payment: The Designer will prepare for the Client, at regular intervals to be agreed upon, certificates authorizing payment to the contractor(s) which will indicate that in the Designer's opinion, based upon the information on the Project available at the time to the Designer, the contractor(s) is (are) entitled to the particular payment in accordance with his contract. Execution of any such certificate by the Designer shall not impose liability on Designer except in the event of Designer's negligence or malfeasance.

2. FEES AND DISBURSEMENTS

2.1 General: The Client shall pay the Designer for his services a fee of:

plus disbursements by or on behalf of the Designer on the Project, other than the Designer's normal overhead, including the following:

Blueprinting:

Reproduction:

Renderings:

Out of Town Travel:

Long Distance Telephone:

Filing Fees:

Other:

2.2 Extra Services: If after a definite scheme has been approved, the Client makes a decision which, for its proper execution, involves extra services or expenses for changes in or additions to the studies, drawings or specifications or otherwise, the Designer shall be paid for such extra services on a design time fee basis of:

2.3 Cost of the Work: Where applicable, cost of the work shall mean the cost to the Client, of the work on the Project and approved extras thereto, including contractor profits and expenses but not including the Designer's and other consultants' fees.

3. PAYMENT OF FEES

Payments of the Designer's fees shall be made as follows:

3.1 Initial Payment: Upon completion of the preliminary studies a sum equal to percent   of the Designer's total fee, computed upon estimated costs of the work or hours to be dedicated by the Designer to the Project.

3.2 Partial Completion: Upon completion by the Designer of approximately percent   of the working drawings and specifications, a further sum sufficient to bring the payment of fees to   percent   of the Designer's total fees, computed upon estimated costs of the work or hours to be dedicated by the Designer to the Project.

3.3 Completion of Drawings: Upon completion of working drawings and specifications to a point where they can be submitted for tender, a sum sufficient to increase payments on the Designer's fees to   percent   of the Designer's total fees computed upon the contract bid or bids approved by the Client (or if no bid has been approved by him then upon the lowest bona fide tender or tenders received) or upon the total hours expected to be dedicated by the Designer to the Project.

3.4 Final Payment: The balance of the Designer's fees or   percent thereof upon substantial completion of Project and all outstanding disbursements.

4. ALTERNATE PAYMENTS OF FEES

4.1 Payments on account of the Designer's fees within the limits above stated shall be made monthly to the Designer in the course of preparation of preliminary studies or working drawings or specifications, or otherwise as has been agreed upon between the Designer and the Client as follows:

4.2 Prepayment: A prepayment of   Dollars ($) on account of the Designer's fees within the limits above stated shall be advanced by the Client at the signing of this contract, or otherwise as has been agreed upon between the Designer and the Client as follows:

5. ADDITIONAL TERMS

The following additional terms form part of this contract:

6. GENERAL

6.1 Effect: This contract shall inure to the benefit of and be binding upon the Parties and, except as herein provided, their executors, administrators, successors and assigns.

6.2 New Partners: If a Party to this contract who is an individual should desire to bring in a partner or partners, or if a Party which is a partnership should desire to bring in a new partner or partners, to share the benefits and burdens of this contract, he or they may do so and he or they will promptly notify the other Party of such action.

6.3 Designer's Property Rights: All drawings, specifications and documents prepared by the Designer are instruments of service for the execution of the work on the Project and are the exclusive property of the Designer, whether the work on the Project is executed or not; and the Designer reserves the copyright therein and in the work executed therefrom and the same shall not be used on any other Project without the Designer's prior written consent and arrangements for compensating the Designer for such use.

6.4 Designer's Responsibility: The Client has the assurances of the Designer that the Designer's services hereunder shall be rendered in good faith and in the professional manner; but the Designer cannot be responsible for the performance, quality or timely completion or delivery of any work, materials or equipment furnished by contractor(s), consultants or others on the Project, or for the accuracy of any cost estimates furnished with respect to the Project, or the ultimate safety and convenience of the persons or entities using the premises with respect to which the "Project" is performed. The Designer may be relieved from his liability for performance of this contract when nonperformance is beyond the control of the Designer.

6.5 Renegotiation: If re-planning of the Project is required as a result of unanticipated budgetary changes, or increased costs due to strikes or acts of God or other unanticipated complexities Designer may request renegotiation of this contract.

6.6 Assignments: Except as above provided, neither Party may assign this contract, or the benefits or burdens hereunder, without the consent in writing of the other Party.

6.7 Governing Law: This contract shall be governed by the laws of the place where the Designer's principal business is located.

6.8 Entire Agreement: This contract supersedes any prior agreements between the Parties and constitutes their entire agreement and understanding on the matters herein covered. No changes, modifications or termination of this contract may be made except in writing signed by the Parties.

7. ARBITRATION

All claims, disputes and other matters arising out of, or relating to, this contract or the breach hereof, which cannot be solved by agreement of the Parties within ten days after the same arise, shall be decided by arbitration in the city (having adequate facilities therefor) where, or nearest to which, the Designer's principal office is located in accordance with the rules of the American Arbitration Association (or such other body as may be mutually agreed at time of execution of contract and as inserted hereafter) then obtaining, unless the Parties mutually agree on some other procedure. Any award resulting from the arbitration shall be final and binding on the Parties and judgment may be entered upon the same in accordance with applicable law in any court of competent jurisdiction. This commitment to arbitrate and any such award shall be specifically enforceable in any such court.

The parties have signed below to evidence their foregoing agreements:

CLIENT:

per

per   Authorized Agent

DESIGNER:
                                 A.S.I.D. Membership #_____
per

per

American Society of Interior Designers

ASID Document 402

Contract for
**Professional Services:
Hourly Rate**

This **CONTRACT** is

made this   day of   in the year of Nineteen
Hundred and

BETWEEN the Client:
(name & address)

and the Designer:
(name & address)

for the following Project:

1. PROFESSIONAL SERVICES

1.1 General: The Designer's professional services shall consist generally of consulting with the Client to determine scope of work; preparing the necessary preliminary studies; making preliminary estimates; preparing working drawings and specifications; advising in the drafting of forms of proposals, tenders and contracts and on proposals and tenders made; instructing or engaging architects, engineers or other special consultants, if required, and incorporating plans and specifications developed by any such special consultants into working drawings and specifications; furnishing to the contractor(s) such copies of the contract drawings and specifications, and detailed drawings to the extent indicated, as are appropriate for the carrying out of the Project; checking of shop drawings when considered appropriate by the Designer; the general observation of the Project; and preparing certificates for payments.

1.2 Preliminary Cost Estimates: The Designer will furnish to or obtain for the Client preliminary estimates of the cost of the Project. If requested the Designer will review, and if required revise, such estimates from time to time as the preparation of drawings and specifications proceeds. Definitive costs can only be expected when contract bids are received.

1.3 Observation of the Work: The Designer will perform or procure such periodic inspections as the Designer may consider appropriate, but constant observation of work on the Project does not form part of the Designer's duties. The Designer will endeavour to warn the Client against defects and deficiencies in the work of the contractor(s), but shall not have responsibility for the failure of a contractor(s) to comply with drawings or specifications or for any latent defect in such contractor(s) work.

1.4 Certificates for Payment: The Designer will prepare for the Client, at regular intervals to be agreed upon, certificates authorizing payment to the contractor(s) which will indicate that in the Designer's opinion, based upon the information on the Project available at the time to the Designer, the contractor(s) is (are) entitled to the particular payment in accordance with his contract. Execution of any such certificate by the Designer shall not impose liability on Designer except in the event of Designer's negligence or malfeasance.

2. FEES AND DISBURSEMENTS

2.1 General: The Client shall pay the Designer for his services, a fee based upon time dedicated by the Designer at the following hourly rates:

plus disbursements by or on behalf of the Designer on the Project, other than the Designer's normal overhead, including the following:

Blueprinting:

Reproduction:

Renderings:

Out of Town Travel:

Long Distance Telephone:

Filing Fees:

Other:

2.2 Cost of the Work: Where applicable, cost of the work shall mean the cost to the Client, of the work on the Project and approved extras thereto, including contractor profits and expenses but not including the Designer's and other consultants' fees.

3. PAYMENT OF FEES
Payments of the Designer's fees shall be made as follows:

4. ALTERNATE PAYMENTS OF FEES
4.1 Payments on account of the Designer's fees within the limits above stated shall be made monthly to the Designer in the course of preparation of preliminary studies or working drawings or specifications, or otherwise as has been agreed upon between the Designer and the Client as follows:

4.2 Prepayment: A prepayment of   Dollars ($) on account of the Designer's fees within the limits above stated shall be advanced by the Client at the signing of this contract, or otherwise as has been agreed upon between the Designer and the Client as follows:

5. ADDITIONAL TERMS
The following additional terms form part of this contract:

6. GENERAL
6.1 Effect: This contract shall inure to the benefit of and be binding upon the Parties and, except as herein provided, their executors, administrators, successors and assigns.

6.2 New Partners: If a Party to this contract who is an individual should desire to bring in a partner or partners, or if a Party which is a partnership should desire to bring in a new partner or partners, to share the benefits and burdens of this contract, he or they may do so and he or they will promptly notify the other Party of such action.

6.3 Designer's Property Rights: All drawings, specifications and documents prepared by the Designer are instruments of service for the execution of the work on the Project and are the exclusive property of the Designer, whether the work on the Project is executed or not; and the Designer reserves the copyright therein and in the work executed therefrom and the same shall not be used on any other Project without the Designer's prior written consent and arrangements for compensating the Designer for such use.

6.4 Designer's Responsibility: The Client has the assurances of the Designer that the Designer's services hereunder shall be rendered in good faith and in the professional manner; but the Designer cannot be responsible for the performance, quality or timely completion or delivery of any work, materials or equipment furnished by contractor(s), consultants or others on the Project, or for the accuracy of any cost estimates furnished with respect to the Project, or the ultimate safety and convenience of the persons or entities using the premises with respect to which the "Project" is performed. The Designer may be relieved from his liability for performance of this contract when nonperformance is beyond the control of the Designer.

6.5 Renegotiation: If re-planning of the Project is required as a result of unanticipated budgetary changes, or increased costs due to strikes or acts of God or other unanticipated complexities Designer may request renegotiation of this contract.

6.6 Assignments: Except as above provided, neither Party may assign this contract, or the benefits or burdens hereunder, without the consent in writing of the other Party.

6.7 Governing Law: This contract shall be governed by the laws of the place where the Designer's principal business is located.

6.8 Entire Agreement: This contract supersedes any prior agreements between the Parties and constitutes their entire agreement and understanding on the matters herein covered. No changes, modifications or termination of this contract may be made except in writing signed by the Parties.

7. ARBITRATION
All claims, disputes and other matters arising out of, or relating to, this contract or the breach hereof, which cannot be solved by agreement of the Parties within ten days after the same arise, shall be decided by arbitration in the city (having adequate facilities therefor) where, or nearest to which, the Designer's principal office is located in accordance with the rules of the American Arbitration Association (or such other body as may be mutually agreed at time of execution of contract and as inserted hereafter) then obtaining, unless the Parties mutually agree on some other procedure. Any award resulting from the arbitration shall be final and binding on the Parties and judgment may be entered upon the same in accordance with applicable law in any court of competent jurisdiction. This commitment to arbitrate and any such award shall be specifically enforceable in any such court.

The parties have signed below to evidence their foregoing agreements:

CLIENT:

per

per

Authorized Agent

DESIGNER:

A.S.I.D. Membership #_____

per

per

2. COMPENSATION AGREEMENT: Presented Price

2.1 For Professional Services as described in Section I, the Designer's Compensation is incorporated in the Presented Price to the Client of all furniture, furnishings, materials and contractual work required to complete the Project. Therefore it is agreed that all furniture, furnishings, materials and labor shall be purchased exclusively through the Designer.

2.2 An advance of $ shall be made by the Client upon execution of this Agreement to compensate for the Design Phases as described in Sections 1.1, and 1.2, and shall be credited to the Client's account at the completion of the Project, but shall not be refundable if the Project is terminated prior to completion.

2.3 No orders for merchandise, materials, and labor will be placed until a purchase order covering same is signed by the Client and returned to the Designer together with payment of   % of the Presented Price. In the event that a source of supply requires total payment in advance the Client will be required to make full payment. After   weeks the Client will be billed for an additional   % of the Presented Price and upon delivery and/or installation of the item(s) the Client will be billed the remaining   %. Invoices are payable upon presentation.

2.4 Any direct purchases by the Client from other sources for implementation of the design work constitutes an exception to this Agreement and is subject to remuneration to the Designer of   % of the purchase price. A copy of the invoice and the Designer's remuneration are to be presented at the time of such purchases.

2.5 The Designer shall notify the Client of any required price increase between time of quotation and placement of order with supplier and will obtain a revised purchase order before proceeding. Approved purchase orders may not be cancelled.

2.6 Orders shall be subject to applicable sales and use taxes, shipping, delivery and insurance in transit. All such costs shall be paid by the Client upon presentation of invoice.

2.7 Disbursements made by the Designer in the interest of the Project shall be billed to the Client. Included in these reimbursements are: ( ) local transportation, ( ) out-of-town transportation, ( ) out-of-town lodging, or $ per diem, ( ) blue prints, ( ) renderings, ( ) long distance telephone calls, ( ) telegrams, ( ) other   . These reimbursements shall be billed to the Client on a ( ) monthly, ( ) semi-monthly basis.

2.8 Should the Client request market trips in addition to those deemed necessary by the Designer, such trips shall be compensated for by the Client at $ per hour for principal, and $ per hour for employees.

2.9 The following additional terms form part of this Compensation Agreement:

This Compensation Form is executed on

CLIENT:

      per

      per

DESIGNER:

      per

      per   A.S.I.D. Registration #_____

ASID COMPENSATION FORM 001 • FOR USE WITH CONTRACT FOR PROFESSIONAL SERVICES: RESIDENTIAL LONG FORM 403 OR WITH RESIDENTIAL SHORT FORM 404   001—1/76

208

2. COMPENSATION AGREEMENT: Hourly Rate

2.1 For Professional Services as described in Section I, the Designer's Compensation shall be computed as follows: Principals' time at the fixed rate of ($) per hour. For the purpose of this Agreement the principals are: Employees' time (other than principals) at dollars ($) per hour.

2.2 Additional services requested by the Client and not covered by this Agreement shall be charged as above.

2.3 An advance of dollars ($) shall be made upon the execution of this Agreement and shall be credited to the Client's account at the completion of the Project. This is the minimum payment under this Agreement and is not refundable if the Project is terminated before completion.

2.4 Disbursements made by the Designer in the interest of the Project shall be billed to the Client. Included in these reimbursements are: ( ) local transportation, ( ) out-of-town transportation, ( ) out-of-town lodging, or $ per diem, ( ) blue prints, ( ) renderings, ( ) long distance telephone calls, ( ) telegrams, ( ) other

2.5 Designer's Charges for Compensation will be billed on a ( ) monthly, ( ) semi-monthly basis, or ( ) other

2.6. The following additional terms form part of this Compensation Agreement:

This Compensation Form is executed on

CLIENT:

per

per

DESIGNER:

per

per   A.S.I.D. Registration #_____

ASID COMPENSATION FORM 002 • FOR USE WITH CONTRACT FOR PROFESSIONAL
SERVICES: RESIDENTIAL LONG FORM 403 OR WITH RESIDENTIAL SHORT FORM 404   002—1/76

---

2. COMPENSATION AGREEMENT: Fixed Fee

2.1 For Professional Services as described in Section I, the Designer's Compensation shall be a fixed fee of dollars, ($).

2.2 An initial payment of dollars ($) shall be made upon the execution of this Agreement. A second payment of dollars ($) shall be made upon completion of the Design Phase. These two payments are the minimum payment under this Agreement and are not refundable if the Project is terminated. A third payment of dollars ($) shall be made upon completion of the Specification and Fabrication Documents Phase. A final payment of dollars ($) shall be made upon substantial completion of the Project.

2.3 For additional services requested by the Client and not covered by this Agreement, Compensation shall be computed as follows: Principals' time at the fixed rate of dollars ($) per hour. For the purpose of this Agreement the principals are: Employees' time (other than principals) at dollars ($) per hour.

2.4 Disbursements made by the Designer in the interest of the Project shall be billed to the Client. Included in these reimbursements are: ( ) local transportation, ( ) out-of-town transportation, ( ) out-of-town lodging, or $ per diem, ( ) blue prints, ( ) renderings, ( ) long distance telephone calls, ( ) telegrams, ( ) other . These reimbursements shall be billed to the Client on a ( ) monthly, ( ) semi-monthly basis.

2.5 If the scope of the Project is changed materially, compensation shall be subject to renegotiation.

2.6 The following additional terms form part of this Compensation Agreement:

This Compensation Form is executed on

CLIENT:

per

per

DESIGNER:

per

per   A.S.I.D. Registration #_____

ASID COMPENSATION FORM 003 • FOR USE WITH CONTRACT FOR PROFESSIONAL
SERVICES: RESIDENTIAL LONG FORM 403 OR WITH RESIDENTIAL SHORT FORM 404   003—1/76

2. COMPENSATION AGREEMENT: Percentage of Project Cost

2.1 For Professional Services as described in Section I, the Designer's Compensation shall be computed on the basis of all items of labor, material and merchandise required to complete the Project, as follows:

       per cent (%) of the cost of Labor,

       per cent (%) of the cost of Furniture, Furnishings and Materials,

       per cent (%) of the cost of Other

2.2 Payment of   dollars ($) shall be made upon the execution of this Agreement. Payment of   dollars ($) shall be made upon completion of the Design Phase. These constitute the minimum payment under this Agreement and are not refundable if the Project is terminated, but the same shall be credited against the payment to be made upon completion of the Specification and Fabrication Documents Phase. Payment of 90% of total compensation shall be made upon completion of the Specification and Fabrication Documents Phase. Balance of total compensation shall be made upon substantial completion of Project.

2.3 For additional services requested by the Client and not covered by this Agreement, compensation shall be computed as follows: Principals' time at the fixed rate of   dollars ($) per hour. For the purpose of this Agreement the principals are:
Employees' time (other than principals) at   dollars ($) per hour.

2.4 Disbursements made by the Designer in the interest of the Project shall be billed to the Client. Included in these reimbursements are: ( ) local transportation, ( ) out-of-town transportation, ( ) out-of-town lodging, or $ per diem, ( ) blue prints, ( ) renderings, ( ) long distance telephone calls, ( ) telegrams, ( ) other   . These reimbursements shall be billed to the Client on a ( ) monthly, ( ) semi-monthly basis.

2.5 If the scope of the Project is changed materially, compensation shall be subject to renegotiation.

2.6 The following additional terms form part of this Compensation Agreement:

This Compensation Form is executed on

CLIENT:

      per

      per

DESIGNER:

      per

      per   A.S.I.D. Registration #_____

ASID COMPENSATION FORM 004 • FOR USE WITH CONTRACT FOR PROFESSIONAL SERVICES: RESIDENTIAL LONG FORM 403 OR WITH RESIDENTIAL SHORT FORM 404

004—1/76

210

TYPICAL INTERIOR DESIGN CONTRACT USED BY HENRY END ASSOCIATES

HEПRY EПD ASSOCIATES

Miami
4100 North Miami Avenue
Miami, Florida 33127
305—576-1670

New York
204 East 58th Street
New York City, New York 10022
212—755-6380

London
4A William Street
London, S.W.I. England
01—235-6312

London, 20 November 1977

Middle East Trading Company
Airport Street
El Kaaki Building
Jeddah, Saudi Arabia

Re: Hotel Design/Planning

Gentlemen:

We are pleased to submit this proposal for professional services:

AGREEMENT

Interior design services for a 350 guest room hotel, 100 apartments and public space, Jeddah, Saudi Arabia.

This Agreement by and between Henry End Associates, having offices at 4A William Street, London, S.W.1, England, hereinafter called "Designer", and Middle East Trading Company, Airport Street, Jeddah, Saudi Arabia, hereinafter called "Client".

WITNESSETH

a. Client is constructing a hotel in Jeddah, Saudi Arabia and hereby retains Designer for complete interior planning and interior design services.

b. Client retains Designer to perform complete design services as is hereinafter set forth, and, in consideration thereof and as compensation for these services, Client agrees to pay Designer such fees as are hereinafter set forth.

SCOPE OF WORK

The Designer will provide the following services:

PHASE I   ESTABLISH PLANNING AND DESIGN DIRECTION

a. Attend and request preliminary conferences for co-ordination with the Architect, the Client, contractor and other parties involved, in order to mutually agree upon general concepts and practical considerations on which to base Designer's initial services as covered by this Agreement.

b. Attend meetings for the purpose of design presentations or project control and co-ordination.

PHASE II   DEVELOP PLANNING AND DESIGN SOLUTIONS

  a. Prepare preliminary studies which will include floor plans, elevations, electrical plans and details, furniture arrangements and decorative elements to include actual samples and/or photographs of fabrics, floor, wall and window treatments, furniture, furnishings and accessories. Preliminary sketches as required to show the anticipated atmosphere.

  b. Present preliminary plans and design concepts for critique with Client.

  c. Upon receipt of Client's approvals, Designer will proceed to complete presentations which will consist of floor plans, actual materials, colour samples and sketches.

PHASE III In conjunction with the above presentations, Designer will provide Client with sufficient information via photographs, tear sheets of manufactured furniture, decorative or special lighting style and types, and floor materials. All pertinent and necessary information will be provided to aid and assist, in order that the Client and the special consultants can commence with their respective responsibilities to provide the architects, contractors and others with production drawings.

PHASE IV   DOCUMENTATION OF APPROVED DESIGNS

  a. Technical Documents

   Based on approved design concepts, prepare complete documentation for all design elements including furniture, furnishings and equipment.

  b. Table of Contents

   List of all drawings applicable to designs and prepare a table of contents to identify each section.

  c. Specifications

   Written specifications where required shall be furnished by Designer and shall include the following:

   1. Materials
   2. Finishes
   3. Dimensions
   4. Construction details, including millwork / joinary and hardware as it is applicable to the approved designs.

  d. Furnish complete design development drawings, including details. Areas not covered sufficiently by written specifications shall be supplemented on the drawings, and may include catalogue cuts and/or actual samples of finish required. In addition, necessary working drawings required, covering such items as electric and telephone locations or other support facilities will be furnished.

  e. Orientation Drawings

   Preparation of complete orientation drawings incorporating finished plans of room or area concerned, showing furniture location, coded to indicate materials and finish (fabric, colour, etc.) and for all items proposed. Where stock items are used, manufacturer's related numbers or identifications will be shown.

f. Upon the completion of the work as outlined in Phases IV
    V, and as part of the purchasing Control Book, a final
    budget predicted upon actual quoted or catalogue prices
    will be prepared and submitted for approval by the Client.
    This budget will act as a guideline for purchasing and
    will be subject to final adjustment.

g. Purchasing Control

    A complete control book will be submitted, which will
    list all items specified with quantitive requirements,
    and shall include type, colour, size, etc. This tabulation
    shall include a consolidated total indicating number of
    units and total tabulation for yardages, where applicable.

h. Special Design

    Selection and/or design of decorative accessories, china,
    silverware, linen, uniforms and all other peripheral
    items affecting the designs. The foregoing is included
    in the fee hereinafter stated.

PHASE V   PURCHASING AND EXPEDITING

    This service is part of the Interior Design scope of work.
    Designer is offering facilities for providing this service
    at 10% (Ten percent) above manufacturer/suppliers ex-factory
    cost, so as to facilitate and expedite this job for Client.

a. Purchase Orders

    Upon written authorization by the Client, the Designer
    will prepare purchase specifications for Client.

PHASE VI   TECHNICAL ASSISTANCE

a. Field Co-ordination

    As required with Client's representative to ensure
    that construction remains on schedule, and that any
    changes required affecting the Designer's work are
    made known and covered in writing.

b. Inspection and Supervision

    At all phases of the construction and installation
    of furnishings to ensure that methods and materials
    conform to the Designer's drawings and specifications.

c. Completion of Work

    Each phase of the Designer's work will commence
    immediately upon Client's direction and will be
    completed prior to such reasonable time as designated.
    All work will be performed pursuant to the instructions
    of the Client and subject to his approval.

FEES

a. Designer's fees for the services outlined above will
    be two hundred and thirty-five thousand (US) dollars.

REIMBURSABLES

Designer and his associates to be reimbursed at actual cost for any out-of-pocket expenses, i.e. travel, food and lodging, long distance telephone charges, telex, cable, blueprinting, etc.

INSTALLATION

a. Designer will provide a representative who will be qualified for on site supervision for Designer's Project work, as required. This representative will be available for site inspections and co-ordination of construction with Designer's drawings. Said representative will be available upon reasonable notice for meetings with the architect, as well as be available for supervision of the installation. All expenses incurred by this representative, i.e. travel, suitable food and lodging, etc. shall be bourne by the Client.

BILLING

Invoices will be submitted as follows:

a. Fifty-five thousand (US) dollars, upon acceptance of this Agreement by Client.

b. Ten thousand dollars (US), every month commencing December 20, 1977 for a period of eighteen months.

GENERAL TERMS

a. Any changes made by Client after approvals, which shall require additional work, shall be paid by Client as an extra charge at the rate of three (3) times payroll.

b. The scope of the work may be modified or expanded, in which case a new Letter of Agreement will be executed so that Client and Interior Designer have a mutually clear understanding of their responsibilities.

c. All items specified by the Designer will be as supplied from the particular manufacturer, wholesaler or dealer, and the Designer makes no warranties or representations expressed or implied of any kind. The Client understands that the Designer cannot be responsible for delays or defaults in the performance of suppliers, dealers, manufacturers or any other persons, but the Designer will work closely with these people in order to ensure their proper performance in every respect.

d. The Client shall provide personnel, space and handling facilities to receive, check and store all deliveries and be responsible for payment of any packing and freight charges, plus applicable taxes and duties.

    The Client, or his contractor(s) shall be responsible to inform the Designer in writing, or any changes affecting the Designer's work in progress.

e. Designer's credits in press releases, advertisements and publicity media, published articles, on site signs and billboards to read as follows:

    INTERIOR DESIGN   HENRY END ASSOCIATES / MIAMI / LONDON

        f. Henry End will personally render his services and meet
            with the Client upon reasonable request.

Your acceptance below will make this proposal the Agreement between us
and authorize the Designer to proceed with the project.

Sincerely,

HENRY END ASSOCIATES

Henry End
President

AGREED AND ACCEPTED:

By   _____
        Authorised Signature by or on behalf of the Client

DATE   _____

TYPICAL IN-HOUSE FORMS USED BY DENNIS JENKINS

DENNIS JENKINS ASSOCIATES
2720 S.W. 28 LANE
COCONUT GROVE. FL. 33133
(305) 444-7431

PROPOSAL

SOLD TO _____
_____
_____
_____

PROPOSAL № 10154
DATE _____
ITEM _____

PROPOSAL

PROJECT _____
AREA _____
CONTROL № _____

DESCRIPTION	QTY	UNIT COST	EXTENSION

INSTALLATION

☐ TOTAL INCLUDES FREIGHT ALLOWANCE
☐ TOTAL DOES NOT INCLUDE FREIGHT
☐ TOTAL DOES NOT INCLUDE ANY HANDLING
   CHARGES. INSURANCE. OR LOCAL DELIVERY

SUB TOT _____
FRT ALLOW _____
PUR FEE _____
TAX ALLOW _____

TOTAL _____
DEPOSIT _____
BALANCE _____

PURCHASE ORDERS FOR ABOVE ITEMS WILL BE ISSUED BY D.J.A
ONLY UPON RECEIPT OF DEPOSIT IN THE AMOUNT SHOWN AND
ONE SIGNED COPY OF THIS PROPOSAL
I AGREE TO THE CONDITIONS ON THE REVERSE SIDE
DATE _____ APPROVED _____

DENNIS JENKINS ASSOCIATES
2720 S.W. 28 LANE
COCONUT GROVE. FL. 33133
(305) 444-7431

INVOICE

SOLD TO _____
_____
_____
_____

INVOICE №
DATE _____
ITEM _____

INVOICE

PROJECT _____
AREA _____
PROPOSAL № _____

DESCRIPTION	QTY	UNIT	UNIT	EXTENSION

INSTALLATION

☐ FREIGHT WILL BE INVOICED AT LATER DATE
☐ COD
☐ NOTES

SUB TOT _____
FREIGHT _____
PUR FEE _____
TAX _____

TOTAL _____
DEPOSIT PAID _____
BALANCE DUE _____

PLEASE MAKE CHECK PAYABLE TO
DENNIS JENKINS ASSOCIATES INC TERMS _____

DENNIS JENKINS ASSOCIATES
2720 S.W. 28 LANE
COCONUT GROVE. FL. 33133
(305) 444-7431

CONTROL

P O № _____
INVOICE № _____
REQUISITION № _____

CONTROL №
ITEM _____
PROPOSAL № _____

CONTROL

PROJECT _____
AREA _____
DATE _____

CAT №	DESCRIPTION	QTY	UNIT COST	EXTENSION
	DIMENSIONS			

FINISH/SPECIAL INSTRUCTIONS

FAB №	DESCRIPTION

WIDTH ☐ INCLUDED
REPEAT ☐ COM. SEE CONTROL SHEET №_____
SPECIAL INSTRUCTIONS

☐ SCOTCHG'D ☐ FIREPROOF'G ☐ BACKG

SOURCE _____
SHIP VIA _____
DATE REQ'D _____
SHIP INSTR _____
SHIP TO _____
☐ BEST WAY   ☐ AIR FREIGHT
☐ FASTEST WAY OTHER THAN AIR

ALLOT	QTY	UNIT COST	TOTAL

BIDDERS	QTY	UNIT COST	TOTAL

SUB TOT _____
PUR FEE _____
SUB TOT _____
TAX _____
FREIGHT _____
TOTAL _____

SEE ☐ BACK ☐ ATTCHED ☐ DJA DRW'G   APPROVED _____

DENNIS JENKINS ASSOCIATES
2720 S.W. 28 LANE
COCONUT GROVE. FL. 33133
(305) 444-7431

WORK ORDER

TO _____
_____
ATTN _____

ARCHITECTONICS
INTERIOR PLANNING
INDUSTRIAL DESIGN

WORK ORDER

DATE _____
JOB _____
SUBJECT _____

AUTHORIZED _____

216

PURCHASE

DENNIS JENKINS ASSOCIATES
2720 S.W. 28 LANE
COCONUT GROVE, FL. 33133
(305) 444-7431

TO _____
_____
_____
ATTN _____

SHIP TO _____
_____
ATTN _____

ORDER

P.O. № _____

DATE _____

TAG _____

DATE REQ'D _____

TERMS _____

F.O.B. _____

SHIP VIA _____
SHIP INST. _____
☐ BEST ☐ AIR ☐ FASTEST OTHER THAN AIR

DESCRIPTION	QTY	UNIT COST	EXTENSION

RESALE № 23-08-147871-36

SUPPLIERS. PLEASE NOTE.
SHOW OUR PURCHASE ORDER № & TAG ON ALL
PACKAGES, INVOICES. & CORRESPONDENCE
INFORM US OF ANY PRICE CHANGE PRIOR TO SHIPMENT
FOR OUR APPROVAL TERMS FROM DATE MERCHANDISE IS RECEIVED
ACKNOWLEDGEMENT OF ORDER & SHIPPING DATE REQUIRED

TOTAL _____
_____
DEPOSIT _____
_____
BALANCE _____

PROPOSAL № _____ APPROVED _____

TRANSMITTAL

DENNIS JENKINS ASSOCIATES
2720 S.W. 28 LANE
COCONUT GROVE, FL. 33133
(305) 444-7431

TO _____
_____
_____
ATTN _____

TRANSMITTAL

ARCHITECTONICS
INTERIOR PLANNING
INDUSTRIAL DESIGN

DATE _____
JOB _____
SUBJECT _____
_____

WE ARE SENDING YOU   ☐ ATTACHED   ☐ UNDER SEPARATE COVER
☐ DESIGN DRAWINGS   ☐ SPECIFICATIONS
☐ DETAIL DRAWINGS   ☐ SAMPLES
☐ SHOP DRAWINGS   ☐ PRODUCT LITERATURE
☐ CHANGES AS NOTED   ☐ _____

№ COPIES	DESCRIPTION	DRWG DATE

THE ABOVE ARE FOR YOUR:
☐ APPROVAL   ☐ ACTION AS NOTED
☐ REVIEW AND COMMENT   ☐ REVISION AS NOTED
☐ RECORD   ☐ _____

COPIES TO _____ ☐ FILE

BY _____

NOTES

PLEASE RETURN ITEMS NOTED TO THIS OFFICE BY _____

IF ENCLOSURES ARE NOT AS NOTED, PLEASE NOTIFY DJA IMMEDIATELY.

Credits

Abu Dhabi Hilton, United Arab Emirats. Architect: Michael Brashier & Associates and Roy Lancaster. Interior designer: Maurice Bailey.

Airport Hotel, Dublin, Ireland. Architect: Stephenson Gibney & Associates. Photographers: John Donat (corridor with court); Norman McGrath (lounge, pool); Henk Snoek Photography & Associates (coffee shop, corridor).

Aladdin Hotel, Las Vegas, Nevada. Architect and interior designer: Lee Linton.

Algonquin Hotel, New York.

Ambassador East Hotel, Chicago, Illinois. Interior designer of the Pump Room: Spiros Zakas. Photographer: Spiros Zakas.

Amstel Hotel, Amsterdam. Photographer: Ben Martin.

Bahrain Sheraton, Bahrain, an island in the Persian Gulf. Architect: Rader Mileto Associates.

Bali Hyatt, Indonesia. Interior designer: Dale Keller Associates.

Balmoral Beach Club, Nassau, West Indies. Architect: John Volk. Interior designer: Henry End Associates. Photographer: Alexandre Georges.

Barbados Hilton, West Indies. Architect and interior designer: Warner Burns Toan & Lundy.

Beverly Hills Hotel, Los Angeles, California. Architect: Welton Becket Associates. Interior designer of ballroom: Pierre Scapula. Photographer: Thelner Hoover.

Hotel Borobudur Inter-Continental, Jakarta, Indonesia. Architect: Sicofrance, Paris. Interior designer: Dale Keller Associates.

Brasilton São Paulo, Brazil.

Bristol Place, Toronto, Canada. Interior designer: Jutras & Nicholson. Photographer: Alexandre Georges.

Caribe Hilton, San Juan, Puerto Rico. Architect: Toro-Ferrer, San Juan. Interior designer: William Boydston.

Carlton Beach Hotel, Bermuda. Architect: William B. Tabler. Interior designer: Henry End Associates.

Carlton Tower, London, England. Architect: Michel Rosenauer, FRIBA. Interior designer:Henry End Associates.

Chosun Hotel, Seoul, Korea. Architect: William B. Tabler. Interior designer: Henry End Associates.

Club Mediterranee, Cancun, Mexico. Architect: Christian de Grand Maison, director of construction for Club Mediterranee. Interior designer: Eric Lieure.

Club Mediterranee, Tahiti. Architect: Christian de Grand Maison, director of construction for Club Mediterranee. Interior designer: Eric Lieure. Photographer: Andree L. Abegassis.

Colonnade, Boston, Massachusetts. Interior designer: Jutras & Nicholson. Photographer: Alexandre Georges.

Contemporary-Resort Hotel, Disney World, Florida. Architect: Welton Becket Associates. Photographer: Walt Disney Productions.

Golden Sands Hotel, Famagusta, Cyprus. Architect: Garnett, Cloughley, Blakemore & Associates, London.

Gulf Hotel, Muscat, Oman. Interior designer: George Wimpey & Co., Ltd.

Habitation Leclerc, Port-au-Prince, Haiti. Architect and interior designer: Larry Peabody.

Hammamet Sheraton Hotel, Tunisia. Architect: Ahrens, Di Grazia, Frizzell of Rome and Chevy Chase, Maryland.

Heathrow Hotel, Heathrow Airport, London. Architect: R. Seifert & Partners. Interior designer: Henry End Associates.

Holiday Inn Bristol, England. Architect: A. J. Hines & Co. Interior designer: Donat J. Burnham & Associates.

Holiday Inn Marble Arch, London, England. Architect: R. Seifert & Partners. Interior designer: Donat J. Burnham & Associates.

Holiday Inn Plymouth, England. Interior designer: Donat J. Burnham & Associates. Photographer: Tom Molland, Ltd.

Holiday Inn Swiss Cottage, London, England. Architect: Dennis Lennon & Partners. Interior designer: Donat J. Burnham & Associates.

Host Hotel, Houston, Texas. Architect: William B. Tabler. Interior designer: Neil Oppenheim.

Howard Hotel, London, England. Architect: Frederick Gibberd & Partners. Interior designer: G. Jackson & Sons, Ltd. Photographers: John Rose & John Dyble.

Hyatt Rama Bangkok, Thailand.

Hyatt Regency Atlanta, Georgia. Architect: John Portman & Associates. Photographer: Pat Canova.

Hyatt Regency Brussels, Belgium. Architect:Hendrick vonden Bosch, Brussels. Interior designer:Henry End Associates. Photographer: Ben Martin.

Hyatt Regency Caspian, Chalus, Iran. Architect: Rader Mileto Associates with Kevin Miller, associate. Interior designer: Henry End Associates. Photographer: Frank Fishbeck of Hong Kong.

Hyatt Regency Chicago, Illinois. Architect: A. Epstein and Sons, Inc. Interior designer: Elster's.

Hyatt Regency Karachi, Pakistan. Interior designer:Henry End Associates.

Hyatt Regency Hong Kong.

Hyatt Regency Manila, the Philippines.

Hyatt Regency Ocho Rios, Jamaica, West Indies. Architect: Rader Mileto Associates. Interior designer: Henry End Associates.

Hyatt Regency San Francisco, California. Architect: John Portman & Associates.

Hyatt Rio Mar, Rio Grande/Luquille, Puerto Rico.

Hotel Inter-Continental London, England. Architect and interior designer: Frederick Gibberd & Partners. Photographer: David Atkins.

Hotel Inter-Continental Maui, Hawaii. Designer: Howard Hirsch & Associates.

Hotel Inter-Continental Mecca, Saudi Arabia. Architect: Professor Rolf Gutbrod of Stuttgart. Interior designer: Jansen of Paris.

Hotel Inter-Continental Riyadh, Saudi Arabia. Architect: Trevor Dannatt, London. Interior designer: Jansen of Paris.

Hotel Inter-Continental Tehran, Iran. Architect: Rader Mileto Associates. Interior designer: Kenneth Smith.

Jerusalem Hilton, Israel. Architect: Rechter-Zarhy-Rechter. Interior designer: Dora Gad. Photographer: Keren-Or.

Kah-Nee-Ta Resort Lodge, Warm Springs, Oregon. Architect: Wolff Zimmer Gunsul Frasca Partnership. Photographers: Ed & Carol Hershberger.

Karachi Sheraton, Pakistan. Architect: Dar-Al-Handassa. Interior designer: Henry End Associates.

Khartoum Hilton, Sudan. Architect: Ali Kolsal. Interior designer: Dale Keller Associates.

Kiawah Inn. Designer: Alan Ferry Designers. Photographer: E. Alan McGee.

Killarney Ryan Hotel, County Kerry, Ireland. Architect: Stephenson Gibney and Associates. Photographer: Henk Snoek Photography & Associates.

Hotel proposed for Kish in the Persian Gulf. Architect: Rader Mileto Associates.

Le Regente Hyatt Montreal, Canada. Architect: David, Boulva, Cleve. Interior designer: Henry End Associates.

Loews Monte-Carlo, Monaco. Architect: Ginsburg, Paris. Interiordesigner: Ellen L. McCluskey Associates.

London Hilton, England. Architect: Sidney Kaye & Partners. Interiors designer: David T. Williams. Photographer: Joe Cocks Studio.

Marco Beach Hotel, Marco Island, Florida. Architect: Vensel, Savage and Associates. Interior designer: Henry End Associates. Photographer: Alexandre Georges.

Margarita Regency Hotel (proposed). Architect: Rader Mileto Associates.

Hotel Marina Palace, Finland. Architect: Jaakko and Unto Rantonen, Helsinki. Photographer: Simo Rista.

Marquette Inn, IDS Center, Minneapolis, Minnesota. Architect: Johnson/ Burgee. Photographers: Bob Porter, Hedrich Blessing (atrium); Philip MacMillan James & Associates (bedroom, corridor).

Marriott Hotel, Cairo, Egypt. Architect: Ahrens, Di Grazia, Frizzell of Rome and Chevy Chase, Maryland.

Mayfair House, New York. Interior designer of Le Cirque Restaurant: Ellen L. McCluskey Associates. Photographer: Henry S. Fullerton III.

Munich Hilton, Germany. Architect: Professor Sepp Ruf in association with Curtis & Davis. Interior designer: Henry End Associates.

Hotel Nacionale-Rio, Brazil. Architect: Oscar Neimeyer. Photographer: Kazmer Takacs.

Nassau Beach Hotel, Nassau, West Indies. Architect: William Bigoney. Interior designer: Henry End Associates. Photographer: Alexandre Georges.

Newport Beach Marriott, California. Architect: William Blurock & Partners and William Kenneth Frizzell. Photographer: Janet Isbell.

Novotel, Coventry, England. Architect: Peter Leather, director of technical services of Novotel (UK), Ltd. Photographer: Richard G. Bailey.

O'Hare Hilton, O'Hare Airport, Chicago. Architect: C. F. Murphy Associates. Interior designer: Norman De-Haan Associates.

Omni International Atlanta, Georgia. Architect: Ventulett & Stainback, Inc. Interior designer: A. W. Jones, Jr., with Genevieve Arnold Alpert (lobby); Jutras & Nicholson (Bugatti Restaurant); Angelo Donghia (French Restaurant and Terrace). Photographer: Alexandre Georges.

Palace Hotel, New York. Architect: Emery Roth & Sons.

Hotel de Paris, Monte Carlo, Monaco. Photographer: Ben Martin.

Peachtree Plaza Hotel, Atlanta, Georgia. Architect: John Portman & Associates. Photographer: Alexandre Georges.

Penta London, England. Architect: R. Seifert & Partners. Interior designer: Henry End Associates.

Hotel Plaza, New York. Architect of original building: Henry Hardenbergh. Interior designer: Henry End Associates. Photographer: Ben Martin.

Rio Inter-Continental, Brazil. Architect: Henrique Mindlin Associates of Rio.

Ritz Hotel, London, England.

Royal Sonesta, New Orleans. Architect: Curtis & Davis. Interior designer of guest rooms: Henry End Associates. Photographer: Alexandre Georges.

The Rye Town Hilton Inn, Rye, New York. Architect: William B. Tabler. Interior designer: Tom Lee, Ltd. in collaboration with Joseph Braswell. Photographer: Alexandre Georges.

Hotel St. Francis, San Francisco. Architect: William L. Pereira Associates. Interior designer: Herbert Bentley. Photographer: Jeremiah O. Bragstad.

The Saint Louis Hotel, New Orleans. Architect: Myrlin McCullar. Interior architect: Richard S. Caldwell Associates. Interior designer; Stephen Gasperecz.Photographer: Frank Lotz Miller.

Saweni Beach Development, Fiji. Architect: Perrett, Lyon, Timlock, Kesa & Associates.

Sheraton Atlanta, Georgia. Photographer: Alexandre Georges.

Sheraton Brussels, Belgium. Architect: Groupe Structure Associates and William B. Tabler. Interior designer: Henry End Associates.

Sheraton Buenos Aires, Argentina. Architects: Sanches Elia, Peralta Ramos, Agostini (SEPRA). Interior designer: Henry End Associates.

Sheraton Dubai, on the Arabian Gulf. Architect: Rader Mileto Associates. Interior designer: Henry End Associates. Photographer: Ben Martin.

Sheraton Park Tower, London. Architect: R. Seifert & Partners. Interior designer: Alan Edwards, Robert Thornton. Photographers: John Rose & John Dyble.

Sheraton Skyline Hotel, London. Architect: Curtis & Davis, with Robert Fielding. Interior designer: original interiors by Henry End Associates, completed by Edwards & Thornton.

Skelligs Hotel, Dingle, County Kerry, Ireland: Architect: Stephenson Gibney & Associates. Photographer: Norman McGrath.

The Stanford Court, San Francisco. Architect: Curtis & Davis. Interior designer:Andrew Delfino. Photographer: Ben Martin.

Tower House, Miami Beach, Florida. Architect: Donald Reiff. Interior designer: Henry End Associates. Photographer: Alexandre Georges(suite); Maris/Seinel (bathroom).

United NationsPlaza Hotel,New York. Architect: Kevin Roche/John Dinkeloo and Associates.

Hotel Villa Magna, Madrid, Spain. Interior designer: Pierre Deshays, Jansen of Paris.

Villars La Rocha, Switzerland (proposed). Consulting architect: Rader Mileto Associates.

The Whitehall, Chicago, Illinois. Architect: Raymond C. Giedraitis. Interior designer: Henry End Associates. Photographer: Alexandre Georges.

Xanadu Yacht & Tennis Club, Freeport, Grand Bahamas. Architect: Charles Giller Associates. Interior designer: Henry End Associates. Photographer: Alexandre Georges.

Selected Bibliography

Books

The Architects Journal, ed. *Principles of Hotel Design.* London: The Architectural Press, 1970.

Architectural Record, ed. *Motels, Hotels, Restaurants and Bars,* 2nd ed. New York: McGraw-Hill, 1960.

Dickens, Charles. *American Notes and Pictures from Italy.* London: Oxford University Press, 1957.

Hamlin, Talbot. *Greek Revival Architecture in America.* New York: Denver Publications, 1964.

Hitchcock, Henry-Russell. "American Influence Abroad" in *The Rise of an American Architecture,* edited by Edgar Kaufmann, Jr. New York: Praeger Publishers in association with The Metropolitan Museum of Art, 1970.

James, Henry. *The American Scene.* New York: Horizon Press, 1967.

Jefferson, Williamson. *The American Hotel, An Anecdotal History.* New York: Knopf, 1930.

Larkin, Oliver. *Art and Life in America.* New York: Holt, Rinehart & Winston, 1960.

Lewis, Sinclair. *A Work of Art.* 1934.

Lundberg, Donald E. *The Hotel and Restaurant Business.* Boston: Cahners, 1974.

Rowntree, Diana. *Interior Design.* London: Penguin, 1964.

Trollope, Frances. *Domestic Manners of the Americans,* edited by Donald Smalley. New York: Knopf, 1949.

Tucker, Gina, and Madelin Schneider. *The Professional Housekeeper.* Boston: Cahners, 1975.

Weisskamp, Herbert. *Hotels, An International Survey.* London: The Architectural Press, 1968.

Periodicals

AIA Journal, July 1975, "Interiors as Architecture—and as a Market."

Architectural Record, February 1976, "Hotels."

Contract, October 1964, "The Sophisticated Means of Henry End Associates."

Contract, April 1975, "Hospitality Remodeling Market Can't Stop for Economy."

Contract, November 1975, Interview with Dale Keller, President of Dale Keller & Associates Ltd., S.A. of Hong Kong, Geneva, and New York.

The Designer, August 1974, "Techniques That Sell Design," by Fran Wilson, AID.

The Designer, March 1975, "Ban the Barriers! Multidisciplinary Teamwork Is Here to Stay!" and "The Unexpurgated Opinions of Eleven Designers."

Domus, July 1971, "Hotel Complex for the Caspian, Iran."

High Life, August 1976, "Hotels & Hotelmanship," by James Cameron.

Hospitality, June 1976, "Coffman on Management"; and "Brener on Finance."

Hotel Management Review, June 1965, "The History of Design & Decor," by Henry End.

Institutions Magazine, November 1969, "The Future."

Interior Design (London), February 1972, Henry End Associates Offices.

Interior Design (London), August 1973, "Creating a Total Ambience," by Sam Stephenson; and "Problems of Hotel Design," by Patrick Garnett.

Interior Design (New York), May 1974, "Lighting the Inner Spaces."

Interiors, July 1969, "Design Firm Case Study of Henry End Associates."

Interiors, December 1974, "The Role of the Lighting Consultant," by David A. Mintz.

Interiors, June 1976, "Vital Signs," by John Follis.

Lighting Design and Application, January 1975, "A Little Light on Sight," by Howard Brandston.

New York, Aug. 9, 1976.

Progressive Architecture, September 1973, "Lighting Design, a Profession Grows," by Howard Brandston.

Saturday Review, Aug. 21, 1976, "America's Most Livable Cities."

Service World International.

Time, March 8, 1976, "Building Fantasies for Travelers."

Time, July 5, 1976, "Downtown Is Looking Up."

U.S. News & World Report, Sept. 8, 1975, "Hotels Shaken by Change—New Names and New Styles."

Index

Numbers in italic indicate photographs.

Edited by Susan Davis
Designed by James Craig
Set in 10 point Century Expanded by Fuller, Inc.
Printed by Halliday Lithograph Corp.
Bound by A. Horowitz & Son